A World of Fine Restaurants in Beijing

Lilian Lee

 FOREIGN LANGUAGES PRESS

First Edition 2008

ISBN 978-7-119-05466-7

© Foreign Languages Press, Beijing, China, 2008

Published by Foreign Languages Press

24 Baiwanzhuang Road, Beijing 100037, China

http://www.flp.com.cn

Distributed by China International Book Trading Corporation

35 Chegongzhuang Xilu, Beijing 100044, China

P.O. Box 399, Beijing, China

Printed in the People's Republic of China

Foreword (1)

In the world of finance or more precisely investment banking, food is a particularly hot topic! The only "fish" we are comfortable with is to fish for companies or businesses! It's the art of the deal rather than the art of the chef that matters! Not in China! The art of the deal is as important as the art of dining. In fact, as my Chinese friends will even say, having a fine dining experience is sometimes as important, if not more important than the deal! A fine dining experience is definitely the prelude to the deal. Or prelude to more deals. Deal origination can then be said to originate from the dining table especially after a few glasses of that deceptively harmless "bai jiu"!!

Over in China, dining is indeed an art form. Here, dining together is more than a gathering of fellow private equity professionals, deal makers or entrepreneurs. It is a social lubricant that builds relationships and strengthens ties that we so often take for granted or overlook. Through my exchange and interactions I have come to realize the real significance of China's food culture! Over here, dining is a process. A journey. Not a destination.

You might ask, "What is that elusive dining experience?" To me, it would encompass aspects that go beyond good food. As you might already find in the culinary capitals of the world, good food is a given, and that is the same in the majestic Chinese capital. A fresh, well prepared and adequately balanced dish of any cuisine is the very basis of this dining experience. An experience which cuts across cultural barriers and dare I say, literally puts differing political viewpoints on the backburner.

Points for this elusive experience stem from a slew of factors, both the tangibles and intangibles. From the decor, ambience, location, quality of service to cutlery, a restaurant's floor plan and table ornaments. The list could go on and on. But as I realize through my treks to the countless Hutongs and restaurants around the city, it is often the smallest of all details that serve as tipping points that takes one beyond a mere culinary experience — but a gastronomical feast beyond the stomach, one that nourishes both the body and the soul while at the same time making the process of dealing and wheeling all the more delectable, if not delicious.

Alas, how often do we all hear expressions like "gosh, the food is just too oily or has a ton of salt!"

This is where my colleague and good friend, Lilian, comes to the rescue. Lilian has brought together a definitive guide of what is currently the best of Beijing i.e. wholesome, healthy and yet delightfully delicious! But like any fast growing metropolis, I would expect Lilian to write revised editions of this guidebook and take both you and I on a journey that sets our senses alight!

Victor Ng- Co-founder &
Group Executive Director of London Asia Capital Plc

Foreword (2)

I have known Lilian for seven or eight years. She has always been an intellectual woman of the new age, who is conscientious toward work and diligent in pursuit of learning. I am familiar with her years of devotion to the protection of the Earth's resources and the natural environment, along with sustainable development of public welfare. I did not discover the gourmet in her until I read Lilian's writings effectively introducing the world's delicacies to be found in Beijing. In particular, her *In the Gourmet Spirit — a World of Fine Restaurants in Beijing* was selected by Chinese publishers for the series, "Good Food for Life Guides for the 2008 Olympic Games," and published in China and internationally in different languages. I really feel happy for her.

Food is a symbol of the culture and economic strength of a country. Attention to and improvements in food, in a sense, demonstrate the enhancement of national culture and progress of social enlightenment. Over the past 30 years of reform and opening-up, China has undergone rapid economic and consumer growth, accompanied by swift development and changes in its food culture, especially in its capital city of Beijing. People from other countries often marvel at and speak highly of dining in China for its increasing diversification, enrichment and delicacies, including the abundant variety in terms of local cuisines.

With a distinguished, all-embracing culture, Beijing has absorbed the many food cultures of the world. Such a diversified gathering of international cuisine is also evidence of the openness and broadmindedness of China. After its successful bid for the 2008 Olympic Games, Beijing became an international metropolis. Through the opportunity of hosting the Olympics, Beijing has become the focus of world attention, with its diversity and gourmet spirit also carrying forward Chinese culture. It is hoped that this book will not only serve as a gourmet's guide, but also introduce to the world, the open harmonious spirit of Beijing and the profoundness of all-embracing Chinese culture.

Hopefully, readers will get a chance to try all the restaurants mentioned in this book and join the "gourmet spirit movement." As Lilian says, "Delicious food is a way of living, and a way of savoring life." With sustainable development of the natural environment attracting greater worldwide attention, we hope that we will be able to join hands and help build an eco-friendly home through our own inner harmony and a gourmet's spirit toward life. We also look forward to the next and even more wonderful books on fine dining in Beijing by Lilian Lee.

Felix Chen
President of Sampo Group

Preface

A modern metropolis as well as historical capital of several ancient dynasties, Beijing is a blending of the old and the new, the East and the West, a fact perhaps best testified by the great diversity of local food. The city displays the cuisines of places from across the country as well as the world, each accompanied by the distinctive setting and service found at their origins. Everyone, whether with a penchant for haute cuisine or home-style cooking, has a choice of delightful places to eat.

I speak from my experience of treating a good number of friends who come to Beijing from all around the globe on business or sightseeing trips. I believe that the question of what, where and how to feed them has much significance in the demonstration of my hospitality. Exulting over my lush offers, many of my pampered pals suggest that I take them to still more restaurants in the city, and press me to promise further pleasant surprises for their palates during their subsequent visits.

In my opinion, one is most impressed by what one eats during a visit to a new place. In this sense, trying out different restaurants in Beijing is a way of learning more about the regions or countries where the cuisines come from. The delight of dining comes to a great extent from ease of mind, graceful settings and exquisite tableware. It is said that only a dish prepared with a sincere heart can truly and fully gratify the diners. The flip side of that is, a diner also cannot truly and fully appreciate a dish without a sincere heart. Good food is not only about good taste, but also about the culture, art and philosophy that lie at its root. Life is not complete without enjoyable food, which nourishes people's stomachs and hearts as well.

I never think of myself as a gourmet, despite the fact that I have visited hundreds of eateries during my six years in the city. But I believe I can give some good advices to those who are keen on dining and wining. I will be only too happy if this book can help enhance the pleasurable stays in Beijing of those who come for the Olympic Games.

I know Beijing through hunting out its diverse cuisines, along with the people and happenings I encounter in the course. That's a process full of pleasant surprises and revelations, during which I become fully involved in local life.

I feel grateful for the many kind suggestions for this book from my friends in and outside of China.

CONTENTS

Choice of Chinese Dishes ··· 1

Top Eight Chinese Cuisines ··· 42

International Cuisines ··· 45

Choice Restaurants ··· 119

China's Renowned Liquors ··· 148

Business Dining ··· 151

Private Dining ··· 173

Seasonal Dietary Regimen ··· 204

Postscript

Acknowledgement

Choice of Chinese Dishes

When for the first time in my life I frolicked on a dining table, I found myself filled with joy as I found full expression for my passion. It is not bad to do something extraordinary every now and again. Don't be afraid of being different, and never hesitate to try something new. Life is an adventure itself.

Da Dong Roast Duck

大董烤鸭

Restaurant Information

Address: 1st and 2nd floor,
Nanxincang International Building,
22A Dongsishitiao（东四十条桥西南
甲 22 号南新仓国际大厦 1-2 层）
Tel: 51690329
Price: average RMB 100 per head
Payment: cash or credit card
Open Hours: 10:00 am to 10:00 pm

In Da Dong's Nanxincang restaurant, customers can watch the whole process of their duck roasting in a stove set right by where you are dining. The decor is imperial, while the food is superior. The best reward for the visit is the roast duck, crispy outside, succulent inside and not greasy. And it can be supplemented by a fine variety of duck

courses, including the unique "Duck Skin in Sugar," which you will not find anywhere else.

Da Dong roasts ducks in an exclusive way, a modification of the traditional method, devised to minimize the loss of nutriments in the roasting process. Customers can find a booklet on every table in the restaurant, instructing them how to match dishes and the appropriate method to eat them.

Specialties

Beijing Duck 北京挂炉烤鸭

Sauteed Duck Heart 火燎鸭心

Ox Tongue with Garlic 蒜子扣牛舌

【Beijing Duck 烤鸭】

Quanjude Roast Duck

全聚德烤鸭

Restaurant Information

Address: 14 Qianmen West Street,
Xuanwu District （宣武区前门西大
街 14 号）
Tel: 63023062
Price: average RMB 150 per head
Payment: cach or credit card
Hours: 11:00 am to 2:00 pm;
4:30 pm to 9:00 pm

Founded in 1864, Quanjude is among the most highly reputed restaurants in China. A visit to Beijing is not complete without trying the roast duck at Quanjude. My favorite is the Supreme Duck, meaty but not oily, emitting the aroma of the fruitwood on which it is baked. Whetting your palate with sips of lemon-soaked water, pick up a piece of hot crispy duck skin, dip it in

sugar, and enjoy its heavenly taste that lingers in the mouth long after slipping down the throat. Over its century-long history Quanjude has developed more than 400 feature dishes, with duck as the centerpiece.

Specialties

Stewed and Seasoned Duck Feet, Liver and Meat 糟溜鸭三白

(This highly nutritious dish is especially valued for its mineral content, being rich in Vitamin A.)

Meat and Tongue on a Nest 雀巢鸭宝

(The dish is a succulent mixture of duck meat, vegetables, pine nuts and peanuts, elegantly arranged on an edible nest.)

Quanjude Roast Duck 全聚德烤鸭

(The dish contains 16 to 25 percent protein, and only 7.5 percent fat, which is mostly unsaturated and low-carbohydrates fatty acids, chemicals that stimulate digestion and vitamin absorption in the human body. Duck fat has a lower cholesterol level than other meats.)

Braised Duck Wings with Broccoli 西兰花鸭翼

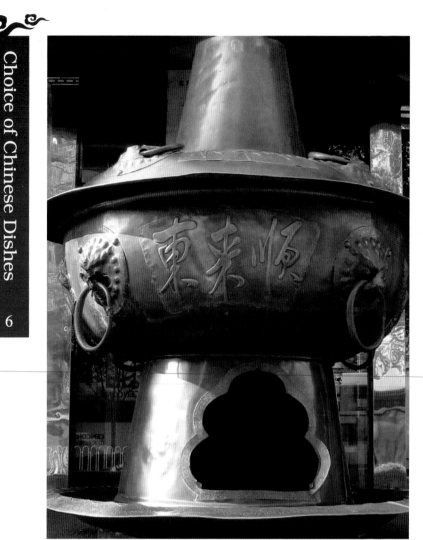

Donglaishun 东来顺

Restaurant Information

Address: 5th floor, Sun Dong'an Plaza, 138 Wangfujing Street, Dongcheng

District（东城区王府井大街 138 号新东安大厦 5 层）

Tel: 65280932

Price: average RMB 60-80 per head

Payment: cash or credit card

Hours: 11:00 am to 10:00 pm

Founded in the early 20th century, Donglaishun is among the best-established brands of dip-boiled mutton in Beijing. The name can be interpreted as "from eastern Beijing with good fortune."

Its lamb is so finely sliced that the blue design of the porcelain plate can be seen through it. Such paper-thin slices are ready for eating after a momentary dip in the boiling shrimp-and-mushroom soup. The restaurant offers a dozen different sauces. And its snacks, such as sweetened garlic and sesame pancakes, are also worth trying.

The chain's headquarters, in the Sun Dong'an Plaza, ingeniously combines its Muslim heritage with the modern style of the shopping center around it. The site consists of both individual rooms of various styles and a spacious common dining area.

Specialties

Dip-boiled Mutton 涮羊肉

Aiwowo 艾窝窝

  (glutinous rice cake with sweet stuffing)

Fried and Simmered Mutton Strips 扒羊肉条

【Sesame pancakes 芝麻烧饼】

【Dip-boiled Mutton 涮羊肉】

Manfulou 满福楼

【Lamb 鲜羊肉】

【Cuttlefish balls 纯鲜墨鱼丸】

Restaurant Information

Address: 38 Di'anmen Street, Xicheng District（西城区地安门内大街 38 号）

Tel: 64030992, 64030993, 64043773

Price: average RMB 50 per head

Payment: cash

Hours: 11:00 am to 10:00 pm

A Muslim restaurant of 15 years, Fumanlou specializes in dip-boiled mutton, beef and seafood. It uses rarely seen purple copper pots, which, when bubbling with milky ox-bone soup, is a real mouth-watering sight. Every serving of sliced lamb is a choice cut. And the cuttlefish balls are made of real cuttlefish flesh plus minced *biqi* (Eleocharis dulcis), which gives it a crispy twist.

Bright red colors well suit the Chinese-themed decor of the setting. The roof balcony, which can be reached by elevator, offers views of the adjacent Jingshan and Beihai parks, both formerly parts of the imperial palace.

Specialties

Lamb 鲜羊肉

Cuttlefish Balls 纯鲜墨鱼丸

Hongyunxuan 洪运轩

【Side dishes 配 菜】

【Lamb 新鲜羊肉】

Restaurant Information:

Address: Ertiao, Shouchang Street,
Beiwei Road, Xuanwu District（宣武
区北纬路寿长街二条）
Tel: 63131914
Price: average RMB 50 per head
Payment: cash
Hours: 11:00 am to 10:00 pm

Hongyunxuan is run by a genial elder who takes delight in regaling customers with stories about dip-boiled mutton. The restaurant is understated in decor, but serves the best lamb at reasonable prices.

Hongyunxuan is distinguished from its peers in that its sliced lamb never leaves stains of blood in the plate and its hotpot soup remains clear throughout the dip-boiling process, both evidence of the top quality of the meat.

Since the sauce becomes diluted after the meat is dipped in repeatedly, the attendants change it regularly to ensure that the flavor is not overpowered. There are several choices of sauce, concoctions including fish sauce, Shaoxing rice wine and a secret mixture of 12 herbs, in addition to the traditional seven ingredients — sesame paste, fermented bean-curd, shrimp oil, pepper oil, sesame oil, flavoring and leek flowers.

Specialties

Lamb 新鲜羊肉
Side dishes 配菜

Yuelu Shanwu 岳麓山屋

Address: Room 10-11, 19A Qianhan
Xiyan, Shichahai, Xicheng District
（西城区什刹海前海西沿甲 19 号）
Tel: 66177978, 66172696
Price: average RMB 83 per head
Payment: cash or credit card
Hours: 11:00 am to 2:00 am

Sitting by Shichahai Lake, the inn offers a superb waterscape encompassed by slender willows, the adjacent Drum Tower and drifting birds. A lure of the restaurant is the loaded bookshelves by the wall, which contribute to the relaxed mood.

The menu includes the best of Hunan dishes. Top is the Fishhead Steamed with Pickled Cayenne. The cayenne is from the mountains of Hunan Province, and preserved in jars before use. The fine-textured fresh fish is thoroughly saturated with the salty hot cayenne sauce, activating each taste bud. After

【Brewed Wild Turtle with Snake 野生水鱼炖蛇】

【Hand-torn Turtle 手撕小鳖】

the fish is done, the leftover spicy sauce can be saved to adorn the noodles, a great-tasting, non-wasteful creation.

The pungent Hand-torn Turtle is made from a secret recipe from Hanshou in Hunan Province. It has to be torn into pieces before being put into the mouth.

Phoenix Pounded Cayenne is reserved for those with the nerve to try the truly hot. Fresh cayenne is baked over a fire, placed in specially designed pots with a sprinkle of salt and garlic, and then served. The customers are instructed to pestle it before tasting. And the harder they pound, the better the mixture tastes.

Tuojiang River White Pepper Shrimp is a reworking of a dish popular among Hunan fisher-men — fried ham and freshwa-ter shrimp with hot and white peppers. The restaurant replaces the river shrimp with greasy-back shrimp, making it taste even better.

Wang Village Grandma's Chicken is a dark-skin free-range chicken stewed with cayenne and ginger. And Taro Rice is rice steamed inside bamboo stalks teeming with taro sauce. The fragrances of fresh bamboo and taro complement and enhance each other.

Specialties

Steamed Fish-head with Pickled
    Cayenne 酱椒蒸鱼头
Nanyue Crisp Bamboo Shoots
    南岳脆笋
Brewed Wild Turtle with Snake
    野生水鱼炖蛇
Hand-torn Turtle 手撕小鳖

Macao Image 濠景轩

【Portuguese-style Egg Tart 葡式蛋塔】

【Portuguese-style Chicken 澳门葡国鸡】

Restaurant Information

Address: At the southern gate of Si De Park, Fangyuan West Road, Chaoyang District（朝阳区芳园西路四德公园南门）
Tel: 64373838, 64389636-819
Price: average RMB 60-100 per head
Payment: cash or credit card
Hours: 10:00 am to 10:00 pm

The restaurant serves fine Portuguese food, and what's more, occasionally hosts healthy-eating lectures, fashion parties and holiday feasts.

Its two-story building, dominated by white, light blue and metal colors, measures up to 3,000 square meters in floorage, and accommodates 30 deluxe private rooms of European design. Wooden multi-leaf screens and cream-colored curtains add a relaxing touch.

Portuguese meals are served in four courses — appetizer, entree, main dish and dessert. My recommendation would be from the Bacalhau series for appetizers, Portuguese-style Chicken, Curry Crab or Portuguese-style Oyster for the entree, Zhuzaibao (piglet pork sandwich) for the main, and then the Egg Tart. And I also never miss the Fried Rice Noodles with Beef or soups during each visit.

Specialties

Portuguese-style Egg Tart 葡式蛋塔
Fried Rice Noodles with Beef
炒牛肉河粉
Portuguese-style Chicken
澳门葡国鸡
Curry Crab 真味蟹
Portuguese-style Oysters 葡式生蚝

Oriental Café Taipan 东方大班

Restaurant Information

Address: 2nd floor, Sunjoy Mansion,
6 Ritan Road, Chaoyang District
（日坛路6号新族大厦2楼）
Tel: 65853478
Price: average RMB 80 per head
Payment: cash
Hours: 11:00 am to 2:00 am

【Poached Mixed Vegetables Portuguese Style
葡式白灼杂菜】

The cafe is as meticulous about its food as its drinks. The Roast Baby Pigeon is well marinated and baked to perfection. The Roast Goose looks shiny with fat, but doesn't taste so. And the great variety of pot soups would deter any attempt to make any quick decisions.

The decor is palpably exotic, with particular attention being paid to details, such as the lightning and fancy doodles on the wall.

Specialties

Curry Beef Brisket 金牌咖喱牛腩
Poached Mixed Vegetables
Portuguese Style 葡式白灼杂菜

Tenggeli-Tala 腾格里塔拉

Address: 1,000m north of Shagoukou, Xicui Road, Haidian District （海淀区西翠路沙沟口北 1000 米）

Tel: 68150808, 68150706

Price: average RMB 200 per head

Payment: cash or credit card

Hours: 11:30 am to 11:00 pm

Website: http://www.tala.com.cn

【Roasted Gigot 生烤羊腿】

Tenggeli-Tala means "pastures in the heaven" in Mongolian. Founded in 2001, the restaurant serves more than 200 classic Mongolian courses, including the famed Genghis Khan Roasted Sheep, served in Mongolian custom as the highest honor for guests. And all the main ingredients are from the grassland and plateaus in northern China.

The dazzling dance drama "Ordos Wedding" is staged every night. There is no better way to experience the enchantment of Mongolian culture than to attend a Mongolian party in a yurt, sipping horse-milk wine while enjoying folk dancing and singing.

The venue patterns itself on mansions of Mongolian nobility, as can be seen from its facade, the yurt-shaped dome, massive studded brass gate and the hammered copper murals.

Specialties

Genghis Khan Roasted Sheep
成吉思汗功勋烤全羊

Princely Grill 王爷烤肉

Roasted Gigot 生烤羊腿

【Princely Grill 王爷烤肉】

Jiumen Snacks 九门小吃

Restaurant Information

Address: Xiaoyou Lane, Houhai, Shichahai, Xicheng District
(西城区什刹海后海孝友胡同)
Tel: 64026868, 64025858
Price: average RMB 20 per head
Payment: cash
Hours: 10:30 am to 1:30 pm, 5:00-9:00 pm

Jiumen Snacks is a courtyard in Houhai where converges a dozen time-honored brand names of Beijing snacks, including Feng's Sheep Tripe, Qian's Rice-cakes, Wei's Yogurt, Yueshengzhai, Ma's Sheep Head, Chen's Pork Intestine, Li's Fried Flour Soup and Dalian Huoshao (pouch-shaped pork and shallot stuffed breads). The food is prepared and served the same way it has always been throughout history, evoking warm memories among senior Beijingers of their early years in the city.

Tea art performances are staged at the Zhangyiyuan Teahouse, another famous brand name in Beijing. There are also assigned stalls with confectioneries and local handicrafts, such as candy-coated haw on a stick, flour figures, clay figures, and papercuts.

The dining space is designed like an old-fashioned family club, with square wooden tables, high-back armchairs, an opera stage, black-and-white photos of scenes from old Beijing, and Chinese ink paintings on tradi-

【Snacks 小 吃】

tional themes. And the private rooms are named after landmarks in the city, such as Qianmen and Chongwenmen. It seems the site is intent on perpetuating the best of the ancient capital city.

Specialties

Various Beijing snacks 北京小吃

【Candied haw on a stick 糖葫芦】

Fengzeyuan 丰泽园

Restaurant Information

Address: 83 Western Street, Zhushikou, Xuanwu District

（宣武区珠市口西大街83号）

Tel: 63186688 ext. 212, 63032828

Price: RMB 100 per head

Payment: cash or credit card

Hours: 11:00 am to 2:00 pm, 4:30-9:00 pm

Fengzeyuan is among the best restaurants providing Shandong cuisine in Beijing. The name implies "big menu and great taste."

The signature course is Sea Cucumber with Shallots, both coming from Shandong Province. With its dark sheen and slippery taste, it is best loved for being rich in protein, low in fat and sugar, and free of cholesterol.

The first floor of the restaurant is the common dining space, which is partitioned by screens. And the second floor has more intimate rooms. Displayed on the eastern wall of the lobby are all the honors the restaurant has received and media stories about it, testifying the niche it has carved for itself in dining and drinking circles in the city and beyond.

Specialties

Sea Cucumber with Shallots 葱烧海参

Soup with Cuttlefish Eggs 烩乌鱼蛋汤

Mandarin Fish in Rice Wine Sauce
糟香桂花鱼

Fish Maw in Chicken Broth 鸡汁鱼肚

【Deep-fried Duck 香酥鸭】

【Braised Beef Tendon in Brown Sauce
红烧牛蹄筋】

Jingucang　金谷仓

【Fish in Chili Sauce 干烧鱼】

【Crispy Duck 仔姜鸭】

Restaurant Information

Address: 1 Northern Street, Sanlitun
(三里屯北街 1 号)
Tel: 64637240, 64637389
Price: average RMB 100 per head
Payment: cash or credit card
Hours: 10:00 am to 11:00 pm

The third branch of Jingucang sits northeast of the German Embassy in northern Sanlitun Street. It can be seen from afar due to its bright orange exterior wall. Ceiling-to-floor windows with western-style drapes, archaic candle-stands, phonographs and dressers from Shanghai and Tianjin make the site a time capsule carrying visitors back to the 1930s. The second floor accommodates four banquet rooms, joined by a balcony that is within arm's reach of the trees.

The food features Sichuan delicacies that locals make only for big occasions or important guests. The ingredients are not expensive, but the cooking process is arduous. The restaurant serves a lovely afternoon tea, and the ice-cream cannot be missed.

Besides the food, customers can buy anything in the restaurant, furniture or ornaments, if they offer the right price.

Specialties

Mouth-watering Chicken 口水鸡
Fish in Chili Sauce 干烧鱼
Brewed Loach 水煮泥鳅
Shredded Pork with Garlic Sprouts
蒜苔肉丝
Crispy Duck 仔姜鸭

Tanyoto 谭鱼头

Restaurant Information

Address: Building 105, Huizhong Beili, Anli Road（安立路慧忠北里105号楼）
Tel: 64848880
Price: average RMB 100 per head
Payment: cash or credit card
Hours: 10:30 am to 11:00 pm

As its name implies, the restaurant specializes in fish-head dishes. This usually ignored part of fish can be amazingly prepared in dozens of ways, such as dip boiled or in chili sauce. The secret of their extraordinary flavors lies in the fish-head, which is exclusively from the fleshy carp species Aristichthys nobilis, and the cayenne, which is appetite stimulating yet not stomach irritating.

In addition to its widely acclaimed fish-head hotpot and crab pot, the restaurant makes a good variety of fine Sichuan dishes. The wide price range makes it possible for people with different budgets to enjoy a hearty meal.

The chain's Yayuncun branch is an impressive business on seven floors that totals 20,000 square meters. Its food indulges the mouth, while the environment and service please the eye.

Specialties

Fish-head Hotpot 鱼头火锅

【Marinated Duck Tongue 卤鸭舌】

【Potherb Pancake 野菜煎饼】

Yuxiang Renjia 渝乡人家

Restaurant Information

Address: 6th floor, Sun Dong'an Plaza, Wangfujing Street, Dongcheng District
（东城区王府井大街138号新东安市场6层）

Tel: 65280668

Price: average RMB 60 per head

Payment: cash or credit card

Hours: 10:30 am to 10:30 pm

The restaurant had no desire larger than presenting its customers with ordinary Chongqing household food at first. The waitresses are mostly from mountainous regions of that city, and share the merits of Chongqing natives, forthright and diligent.

The dining space is decorated with items of daily use from Chongqing's countryside, such as well-pulleys and stoves. And the private rooms are designed like farmhouse interiors, with paintings on the walls, tablecloths and tableware all of rustic designs.

The food fits in well with the unpretentious style of the setting. The snacks and entrees are all familiar names, such as Dandan Noodles, Spicy Noodles, Steamed Stuffed Bun, Yu-Shiang Shredded Pork (Sauteed with Spicy Garlic Sauce), Chicken Cubes with Peanuts, and Mapo Tofu (Stir-Fried Tofu in Hot Sauce). And their taste is 100 percent Sichuan.

Specialties

Boiled Fish Fillet in Fiery Sauce 水煮鱼

Shredded Pork with Garlic Sauce 鱼香肉丝

Chicken Cubes with Peanuts 官保鸡丁

Mapo Tofu 麻婆豆腐

Chongqing Mixed Vegetables 渝乡拌菜

Dandan Noodles 担担面

Spicy Noodles 麻辣面

Fanqian Fanhou 饭前饭后

Restaurant Information

Address: Granary A13, 22 Nanxincang, Dongsi Shitiao, Dongcheng District
（东城区东四十条南新仓 22 号古仓群 A13）
Tel: 64059598, 64096978
Price: average RMB 80 per head
Payment: cash or credit card
Hours: 11:00 am to 11:00 pm

The name is catchy in Chinese, meaning "before and after the meal," though more obscure in English translation. The food includes classic Taiwan gastronomy and recipes contributed by big stars in the entertainment industry.

The Taiwan Sausage is sweetish, smooth yet not greasy. The Pepper Shrimp is a deep-fried item, but not the least heavy; the shrimp bursts fresh out of the crisp shell at the lightest bite, releasing a strong flavor of pepper.

The restaurant is nestled in a 600-year-old imperial grain depot, accommodated in one of the ancient barns itself. The site still keeps the dilapidated ceiling and peeled outer wall of the old structure. Plants in clay pots by the ground-floor windows and frolicking fish in the giant urn at the gate are signs of the undying vibrancy of the time-weathered building, which silently teaches the lesson — everyone is unique in the world, and everyone should be a brave self.

Specialties

Taiwan Sausage 自制台湾香肠

Pepper Shrimp 胡椒虾

Molin Mutton Ribs 默林羊排

【Pepper Shrimp 胡椒虾】

【Steamed Fish 家乡蒸鱼】

【Marinated Pig Trotters 卤猪脚圈】

【Taiwan Sausage 自制台湾香肠】

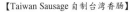

Shin Yeh 欣叶

Restaurant Information

Address: 6 Gongti West Road,
Chaoyang District （朝阳区工体西路
6 号）
Tel: 65525066
Price: average RMB 80 per head
Payment: cash or credit card
Hours: 11:00 am to 11:00 pm

Under the emblem of two dancing leafs, which implies life and prosperity, Shin Yeh has been operating in Taiwan for 28 years, and is now expanding out of the island.

Its menu combines classic Taiwan courses with innovative touches. And unique flavors are guaranteed through the use of secret family recipes with indigenous Taiwan produce.

The setting is unpretentious, with western tinges. The 12 private rooms are named after 12 scenic cities and resorts in Taiwan. And the common dining section, with a capacity for

【Kidneys with Sesame Sauce 麻油双腰】

【Steamed Shark's Fin and Mixed Meat 台式佛跳墙】

【Sweet Almond Pudding 杏仁豆腐】

80 people, is named "Yushan," after the highest peak in the island. Its wall is lined with large photographs of the places the private rooms are named after, creating a perspective of outlook-points from the top of the peak.

Specialties

Roast Pigeon 脆皮乳鸽

Kidneys with Sesame Sauce 麻油双腰

Nine-hole Refreshment 如意九孔

Steamed Shark's Fin and Mixed

Meat 台式佛跳墙

Sweet Almond Pudding 杏仁豆腐

【Nine-hole Refreshment 如意九孔】

No. 4 Kitchen 四号厨房

【Hainan Chicken Rice 海南鸡饭】

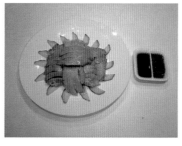

Restaurant Information

Address: 1st floor, Building No. 7,
Soho, Jianwai Street, Chaoyang District
（朝阳区建外 SOHO 7 号楼 1 层）
Tel: 58693844
Price: average RMB 50 per head
Payment: cash
Hours: 11:30 am to 10:30 pm

The restaurant focuses on four cuisines — Shanghai, Taiwan, Singaporean and South Korean. It appeals to naturalists, with a menu easy on oil and salt and free of monosodium glutamate.

When my stomach itches for Hainan Chicken Rice, I know it is time to visit the No. 4 Kitchen. Prepared with chicken meat, broth and rice, the dish brings out the best of the original savory of the ingredients. It's said that the chefs work with a quota of 55 chickens every day, and take only the drumsticks for the dish. If you don't get a reservation for it at dinnertime, you can do no more than but get whiffs of it from the neighboring tables.

The moderate-sized restaurant features elegant, simple decor. Posh tableware and crystal chandeliers add style to the site. Among the regulars are many celebrities. The owner has reserved one wall for their photos and signatures.

Specialties

Hainan Chicken Rice 海南鸡饭
Sauteed Beef Fillet with Black
  Pepper 黑椒牛柳
Red-bean Ice 红豆冰
Fried Pork Chop 香酥小煎猪排

【Crown Daisy Mixed with Dried Tofu Cubes 茼蒿菜拌香干】

Gaisang Medog 格桑梅朵

【Shangri-La Clay Hotpot 香格里拉土陶火锅】

【Roasted Lamb Ribs 烤羊排】

Restaurant Information

Address: Southwest of the Xindong
intersection, Dongzhimenwai Street,
Chaoyang District（朝阳区东直门外
大街新东路十字路口西南角）
Tel: 64179269
Price: average RMB 100 per head
Payment: cash or credit card
Hours: 11:00 am to 11: 00 pm

"Gaisang medog" is a Tibetan
phrase expressing best wishes, a
blessing the proprietor extends
to all visitors. Behind its gate,
with handmade brass ornaments,
is a restored Tibetan home full
of typical Tibetan things, including prayer wheels, hada (white
auspicious scarves), Thangka
(scroll paintings) and folk music.
The staff, all dressed in Tibetan
robes, attends to customers with
warm smiles and marvelous
patience. The climax of the experience is the circle dance in
which all present participate. It
is a moment of revelry when all
sadness disappears, and everyone has the feeling of dancing at
the entrance of Shangri-La.

Specialties

Shangri-La Clay Hotpot
香格里拉土陶火锅
Shangri-La Tibetan Ham
香格里拉藏猪腊肉
Barley Wine 青稞酒
Buttered Tea 酥油茶

Makye Ame 玛吉阿米

Address: 2nd floor, Jinhuyuan Apartments, 23 Baijiazhuang Dongli, Chaoyang
District（朝阳区白家庄东里23号锦湖园公寓会所2层）
Tel: 65088986
Price: average RMB 60 each for lunch, and RMB 100 for dinner
Payment: cash or credit card
Hours: 11:30 am to 1:00 am
Performances (two): 8:00-10:30 pm

There is a household poem in Tibet: "When the bright moon climbs above the airy mountains in the east, the sweet smiles of Makye Ame come to mind." Makye Ame is a goddess synonymous with motherhood and purity to the Tibetan people.

The restaurant lobby is adorned with antique colorfully painted furniture and artifacts from Tibetan households and temples, such as bronze incense burners and jars to hold "holy water." The shelves are stacked with books on various Tibetan topics. But the real eye-catcher is the 6m-long Buddhist horn instrument on the wall. The bar, Buddhist shrines and beams all bear magnificent carvings of traditional Tibetan craft. Old-fashioned paper lanterns hang down the window, and a wool tapestry about "a burning treasure map" hangs grandly at the end of the corridor.

My favorite dishes in the restaurant are the Roasted Lamb Ribs with a secret-recipe sauce, Fried Beef with Tibetan Pickled Radish, and Yak Meat Fried with Pickled Turnip and Cayenne, served together with thin pancakes. The quaintly named Palak Paneer is actually spinach paste with yogurt curd. The must-try item in the dessert category is the Droma Salad, a mixture of eight fruits and vegetables,

including the nourishing Potentilla anserina Linn, concocted with a yogurt sauce made through natural methods.

During the meal singers will come to each table, presenting a song of good wishes and hada or auspicious white scarves. The restaurant stages a Tibetan-styled cabaret at 9 pm every night, during which the customers are invited to participate.

Specialties

Roasted Lamb Ribs 草原生烤羊排

Palak Paneer 巴拉巴尼

Droma Salad 酸奶人参果八宝色拉

Fresh Home-brewed Barley Wine
青稞鲜酿

【Fresh Home-brewed Barley Wine 青稞鲜酿】

【Palak Paneer 巴拉巴尼】

Afanti's Hometown Cabaret

阿凡提家乡音乐餐厅

Afanti is a witty man steeped in the folklore of the Xinjiang Uygur Autonomous Region. The restaurant makes wonderful kebabs. Another signature dish is the roasted whole sheep, which is sliced in front of customers by the chef. Prepared over a long and complicated process, the meat, crispy outside and juicy inside, ensures a heavenly taste with each bite.

The eating space is occupied by dozens of rows of iron tables, which every night serve as the stage after all the dishes are cleared and tables are wiped off. Customers are encouraged to join the Xinjiang dancers on the table. Few will refuse, as the wild abandon and romance of the culture from the deserts and prairies is so contagious.

When for the first time in my life I frolicked on a dining table, I found myself filled with joy as I found full expression for my passion. It is not bad to do something extraordinary every now and again. Don't be afraid of being different, and never hesitate to try something new. Life is an adventure itself.

Specialties

Roasted Sheep Leg 烤羊腿
Roasted Beef with Lemon
　柠檬烤牛肉

Restaurant Information

Address: A2 Guaibang Hutong, 188 Chaonei Street, Chaoyang District (朝阳区朝内大街188号拐棒胡同甲2号)

Tel: 62186060

Price: average RMB 100 per head

Payment: cash, check or credit card

Hours: 11:00 am to 11:00 pm

Show Times: 7:45-8:30 pm 8:45-9:30 pm

Tabletop carnival: 9:30 pm to closing

【Roasted Sheep Leg 烤羊腿】

【Roasted Beef with Lemon 柠檬烤牛肉】

Jia 21 Guesthouse 甲21号

【Sour and Hot Shrimp 酸辣生虾】

【Nanmi Wild Vegetables 喃咪野生菜】

Restaurant Information

Address: A21 Beitucheng East Road, Chaoyang District（朝阳区北土城东路甲21号）

Tel: 64895066

Price: average RMB 80 per head

Payment: cash or credit card

Hours: 11:00 am to 11:00 pm

【Countryside Carp 乡村鲫鱼】

Specialties

Miao-style Sour Fish Soup 苗家酸汤鱼

Folk Seafood Soup 民族海鲜汤

Nanmi Wild Vegetables 喃咪野生菜

Steamed Pot Chicken 汽锅鸡

Sour and Hot Shrimp 酸辣生虾

Countryside Carp 乡村鲫鱼

The restaurant is a blend of the traditional and the vogue. It is a compound including a courtyard and a rear patio that is encircled by metallic walls. The towering trees, casting cool shade, make it an ideal place to have a beer on hot summer days.

The menu encompasses exotic dishes from Yunnan, Guizhou, Thailand, Myanmar and Vietnam, which are similar in flavor. The restaurant calls this wide-ranging collection "Jia food."

Jia food is rich in fish sauce, curry, knotweed and tomato. Many of the ingredients are flown in from their places of origin, to ensure the best flavor. Some courses are spicy, but mildly and pleasantly so.

One Night in Beijing 北京一夜

Restaurant Information

Address: B1 floor, Jinglun Hotel, 3 Jianwai Dajie Street, Chaoyang District（朝阳区建外大街3号京伦饭店 B1 层）

Tel: 65079778

Price: average RMB 80 per head

Payment: cash or credit card

Hours: 11:00 am to 2:00 am

Specialties

Cocktails 鸡尾酒

Roasted Fish 烤鱼

【Cocktails 鸡尾酒】

Located in the five-star Jinglun Hotel, One Night in Beijing molds itself to fit nicely with the location's classic European style. Dazzling chandeliers, plush sofas, paintings from various schools, dim candlelight and soft music, all whisper the message "take your time and enjoy the moment."

The food is focused around Yunnan cuisine with innovative touches, going beyond to the cuisine of neighboring countries such as Vietnam and Thailand. Food is what the restaurant is all about, and everything tastes even greater when the mood and environment are right.

Sit and Forget 一坐一忘

Restaurant Information

Address: 1 Beixiaojie Street, Sanlitun
（三里屯北小街1号）
Tel: 84540086, 64675235
Price: average RMB 50 per person
Payment: cash
Hours: 10:30 am to 11:00 pm

I was first pulled in by the restaurant's fancy name, and became even more fascinated when walking around inside. It serves self-brewed Dai (ethnic group) rice wine, a sour sweet light beverage that always adds

【Steamed Perch with Lemon 柠檬蒸鲈鱼】

a blush to my cheeks and dizziness to my head. The Sulima wine of the Mosuo people is even stronger. Brewed with spring water from the Yulong Snow Mountains, it is a drink reserved for local weddings. A dose of water with lemon will enhance its flavor.

Basking in warm sunshine by the window and receiving a Lijiang wheat-cake from a smiling Naxi young woman, one may feel as if one were relaxing in the beautiful and peaceful land of Yunnan, the province of the cuisine.

The restaurant serves various Yunnan teas. One worth recommending is "Green Mountains and Rivers," a green and slightly bitter plant that grows by the Jinsha River. It is said to be able to alleviate negative heat from the human body. Another special tea is "Three Courses Tea," bitter, then sweet, followed by mellow. The three courses of tea is meant to imply the life course. Bai people present the drink to their most distinguished guests.

The lobby is lavishly adorned with pictures of Lijiang, an ancient city in Yunnan Province. The decor is of authentic Naxi style, as is displayed by the massive wood tables and chairs and lamps of handmade paper.

Specialties:

Banna Wine in Bamboo Barrel 版纳竹桶酒

Chilled Purple Asparagus 冰镇紫芦笋

Beef with Mint and Lemon 薄荷柠檬牛肉

Pot Rice Noodles 罐罐米线

Lijiang Wheat-cakes 丽江粑粑

Lijiang Chickpea Curd 丽江鸡豆粉

Steamed Perch with Lemon 柠檬蒸鲈鱼

【Banna Wine in Bamboo Barrel 版纳竹桶酒】

【Chilled Purple Asparagus 冰镇紫芦笋】

【Lijiang Chickpea Curd 丽江鸡豆粉】

【Beef with Mint and Lemon 薄荷柠檬牛肉】

Tea-Horse Ancient Road

茶马古道

Restaurant Information

Xiandaicheng Branch

Address: 3rd floor, Building D, SOHO New Town, 88 Jianguo Road, Chaoyang District (朝阳区建国路 88 号 SOHO 现代城 D 座三楼会所)

Tel: 85804286, 85804120

Tianhefang Branch

Address: Unit 12 and 13, A19 Xiyan, Qianhai, Shichahai, Xicheng District (西城区什刹海前海西沿甲 19 号单元号 12、13 号)

Tel: 66155515

Price: average RMB 80 per head

Payment: cash or credit card

Hours: 10:30 am to 2:00 am

This was a passage of trade between China and Nepal and India that first appeared over 2,000 years ago. Caravans on horses commuted along it to exchange Chinese tea with silver, gold, furs and herbs from neighboring countries; thus came the name "Tea-Horse Road." The namesake restaurant has a niche in Beijing's dining sector for its Yunnan cuisine and artistic flavors.

Its Mushroom Soup is a gem in the menu. A mixture of more than 40 species of wild mushrooms from the Yunnan and Tibetan plateaus are pot-brewed with a secret recipe that maintains the mushrooms' nutritive value and swells their flavors to a sublime point.

The restaurant is a modernistic structure of steel, wood and glass in their original hues. Artworks and albums are displayed regularly on the site, offering a visual feast and easing the mood of visitors ruffled by daily occupations.

【Pork with Mustard Root and Cayenne 乳扇金针荼香虾】

Specialties

Pork with Mustard Root and
Cayenne 乳扇金针荼香虾
Steamed Pot Chicken 汽锅鸡
Rice Noodle 过桥米线
Mushroom Soup 菌香汤火锅

【Steamed Pot Chicken 汽锅鸡】

【Banana Leaf Roast Fresh Mushroom 蕉叶烤童茸】

Kong Yiji 孔乙己

Restaurant Information

Address: Southern shore of Houhai, Denei Street, Xicheng District（西城区德内
大街后海南岸）

Tel: 66184915

Price: average RMB 80 per head

Payment: cash or credit card

Hours: 10:00 am to 2:00 pm; 5:00-10:00 pm

The homey exterior of the Kong Yiji belies its intriguing interior. At the end of a cobble path behind the black gate stands a house with gray-tiled roof and wooden windows. The tables are covered with batik white-and-blue cloths. Curtains and wooden screens are scattered through room in a casual yet well-conceived manner. The effect is reminiscence of an old-time pub in regions south of the

Yangtze River.

The food is of Shaoxing cuisine, which extensively uses freshwater fish and shrimp, poultry and tofu, and stresses the original flavors of the ingredients. Easy on oil and free of hot pepper, the food is well cooked in rich sauces. The preserved meat goes exceptionally well with fresh vegetables in the stewed or steamed entrees, and a dose of Shaoxing rice wine best enhances the mellow savoring. I especially love the wine. The Soup with Dried Cabbage and the Freshwater Shrimp have the very taste you can find in Shaoxing.

After indulging on the classic southern Chinese food, customers can take their time sipping green tea in the restaurant's small patio, where gold fish wend their way through the pond and bam-

boo leaves rustle with each breeze. These are moments of genuine peace and simple happiness.

Specialties

Fennel Beans 茴香豆

West Lake Vinegar Fish 西湖醋鱼

Dongpo Pork 东坡肉

Soup with Dried Cabbage

Freshwater Shrimp 干菜河虾汤

【Fennel Beans 茴香豆】

【Fried Bean Curd 炸响铃】

Top Eight Chinese Cuisines

The broad diversity of China's geographical conditions, climate and local produce has contributed to the development of eight major cuisines across the country. These are the cuisines of Shandong, Sichuan, Guangdong, Hunan, Fujian, Jiangsu, Zhejiang, and Anhui.

Shandong Cuisine

Developed on the basis of local culinary styles around Jinan and the Jiaodong Peninsula, Shandong Cuisine is best known for its seafood dishes. It emphasizes the maintenance of the original taste of the ingredients and is particular about soup-making. A soup should either be clear or thick: a clear soup should be transparent and palatable, and a thick soup should be milky and smooth.

(Representative Restaurants: Jingya, Fengzeyuan)

Sichuan Cuisine

It has a long history and incorporates local cooking styles of Chengdu and Chongqing. Sichuan Cuisine is known for its preference for its hot and spicy seasonings.

(Representative Restaurants: South Beauty, Yu Xiang Ren Jia, Jin Gu Cang, Tanyoto, Huangcheng Laoma, and Great Wall Hotel 21st Floor)

Guangdong Cuisine

Incorporating Guangzhou, Chaozhou and Dongjiang culinary styles, Guangdong Cuisine uses a wide diversity of cooking ingredients and features lightness and freshness in taste. Guangzhou dimsum is famous across China and internationally. It both looks and tastes great.

(Representative Restaurants: Tang Gong Haixian Fang, China World Hotel Summer Palace, Peninsula Beijing, Noble Court, Gloria Plaza Hotel Sampan Restaurant, Gourmet Room, China Lounge, House by the Park, and Santosa)

Hunan Cuisine

The intense use of red and green hot peppers distinguishes Hunan Cuisine. Its fancy knifework is also very impressive, such as in its hair-thin tripe.

(Representative Restaurant: Yuelu Shanwu)

Fujian Cuisine

It is known for its skill in maintaining original tastes in dishes, in both their sauces and ingredients. Most Fujian dishes are soupy. They are light in taste with a bit of sweetness and sourness.

Jiangsu Cuisine

It excels in cooking freshwater aquatic products. It is particular about maintaining their fresh taste and seasoning the stock to produce wonderful flavors. Jiangsu desserts are also very delicious, which those with a sweet tooth should not miss.

(Representative Restaurant: Su Zhe Hui)

(Merrylin and Lu Lu Restaurant also fall into this category, though they are Shanghai cuisine)

Zhejiang Cuisine

Incorporating Hangzhou, Ningbo and Shaoxing cooking styles, Zhejiang cuisine is also known for its fish and shrimp dishes, since the area is abundant in freshwater aquatic products. Like the famed local women, Zhejiang dishes are considered delicate and exquisite.

(Representative Restaurants: Zhang Sheng Ji, Wahaha Restaurant, and Kong Yiji)

Anhui Cuisine

It stresses the use of nature-blessed and healthy ingredients, and promotes dietary therapy as a way of staying healthy.

International Cuisines

I find that being happy is like a habit. The sense of happiness comes from an easily contented and appreciative heart, rather than from deep pockets. I decided to enrich my life through searching for good food in the world, and remain happy every day.

Pili Pili 比力必利非洲风情餐吧

Restaurant Information

Address: Xingba Road, Nürenjie,
Chaoyang District（朝阳区女人街莱
太星巴路）
Tel: 84484332, 84483372
Price: average RMB 80 per head
Payment: cash or credit card
Hours: 10:00 am to 2:00 am

It is the first and only African restaurant in Beijing. The name "Pili Pili" is an African way of saying "chili," and is meant to appease the homesickness of African sojourners in the city.

The thatched construction

stands out in a district crammed with modern skyscrapers. The interior resembles a miniature African art museum. And all items on display are open for purchase. It sets up a sightseeing platform and an open-air grill section by a flowing stream, both ideal sites for parties and group activities.

The food emphasizes Egyptian cuisine, dominated by chicken, fish, mutton and beef, all lavished with chili and tomato sauce. Every month Pili Pili stages promotions for different dishes, and publishes chef's recommendation items, which are great help for first-time visi-tors to the African restaurant.

The business has joined hands with African embassies in Beijing to host cultural weeks dedicated to one African country each month. And bands of African performers and Arabic singers and dancers perform on the site every day.

Specialties

Kenyan-style Hunting Steak
肯尼亚风味狩猎牛排
Plipli Soup 比力必利汤
RST Mixed BBQ Plate 菜索托什锦烧烤
Black Pepper Noodle with Beef
黑椒柳丝炒面

【Black Pepper Noodle with Beef 黑椒柳丝炒面】

【RST Mixed BBQ Plate 菜索托什锦烧烤】

1001 Nights 一千零一夜

Restaurant Information

Address: Opposite the Zhaolong Hotel, Gongti North Road, Chaoyang District
（朝阳区工体北路兆龙饭店对面）

Tel: 65327243, 65324050

Price: average RMB 60-70 per head

Payment: cash, credit card or check

Hours: 11:00 am to 2:00 am, Arabic art performances from 8:00-10:30 pm

Website: www.1001nights.com.cn

The restaurant opens a door to fantastic Syrian-Lebanese cuisines as well as enchanting Arabic culture.

The facade is impressive, with six enormous arch gates, each adorned with a glass painting depicting a *1001 Nights* tale. The dining space resembles an Arabic castle. Sumptuous sand carvings on the walls, the arched ceiling, gorgeous chandeliers and Arabic-fashioned ornamentals all create a powerfully eye-catching setting.

Hummus bi Tahini is a popular Arabic appetizer. Hummus, made from indigenous chickpeas in Arabic countries, is macerated, grounded, and prepared with spices, lemon extract and olive oil.

The 1001 Nights Grill is an artfully stacked pile of 14 grill items, including beef, mutton and chicken kebabs. Falafel and Fried Kibbeh include two parts: the former is a deep-fried Hummus bean course, followed by dried dumplings stuffed with pine nuts and minced mutton, wrapped in wheat flour with lemon extract.

Specialties

Hummus bi Tahini 胡木思酱

1001 Nights Grill 烧烤夜

Falafel 飞来飞

【Hummus bi Tahini 胡木思酱】

【Tabbuli 塔布理】

【Lady Fingers 指头卷】

Fried Kibbeh 炸卡宝

Tabbuli 塔布理

Antably Kebab 恩嗒批黎卡巴

Shukaf (lamb skewer) 隔山肉串

Lady Fingers 指头卷

【Shukaf (lamb skewer) 隔山肉串】

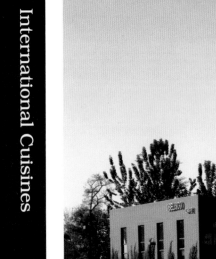

Obelisco 阿根廷烤肉

Restaurant Information

Address: 1 Laiguangying East Road, Chaoyang District （朝阳区来广营东路 1 号）

Tel: 84701666, 84701888, 84703828

Price: average RMB 80 per head

Payment: cash or credit card

Hours: 11:30 am to 11:00 pm

Website: www.betc-obelisco.com

The premises are composed of four parts: grill section, cafe, Obelisco, and a wine cellar with a capacity for 40,000 bottles. The grill, the wine and the service are all typically South American.

Its grilled beef is marinated with a special sauce and roasted over a charcoal fire, essential to preserving the moisture and fine texture of the meat. Argentine diet is heavy on grilled meat. As a counterbalance, locals also

consume large volumes of fresh vegetables and drink a special tea called Mate, which can rinse the fat cells from blood vessels and expel "evil heat" from the human body. Wine is also an inalienable part of Argentine meals. Local-produced wine is sweeter than those from other parts of the world, as the abundant sunshine in the nation has blessed its grapes with higher sugar content.

Specialties

Argentinean Empanada

阿根廷"恩巴纳达"（特色大馅牛肉丁角）

Del Litoral Salad 阿根廷河岸沙拉

Grilled Boneless Chicken Seasoned

with Oregano 风味烤鸡腿

Beef Bone Ribs 烤带骨腹肉

Prawns Fried in Chili, Garlic, Parsley

and Olive Oil 陶盏蒜茸大虾

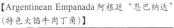

【Argentinean Empanada 阿根廷"恩巴纳达"（特色大馅牛肉丁角）】

Morel's 莫劳龙玺

Restaurant Information

Address: 27 Liangmaqiao Road,
Chaoyang District, 300m east of
Kempinski Hotel（朝阳区亮马桥路
27号）
Tel: 64373939
Price: average RMB 100-200 per head
Payment: cash or credit card
Hours: 11:30 am to midnight

【Belgian Beef 比利时烩牛肉】

Across Belgium every village has breweries that can make some of the world's best beers. More than 50 Belgian beers appear in Morel's drink list, including several of fruit flavors favored by ladies, as well as the world's only six beers brewed by churchmen using traditional methods.

Pot Mussels Cooked in Grandmother's Style is a masterpiece of the Belgian bistro. With a sprinkle of onion, celery and seasoning, it gives prominence to the natural flavor of the mussels. Steak Tartar Pure Tenderloin boasts top-grade beef with Jamaican pepper, and has won top cuisine prizes in Beijing for three successive years. The savory Holland Maatjes with Mixed Salad is steamed with potato to smooth over the briny seafood odors.

Green curtains, blue tablecloths, an antique French-fries cutter and Dutch wooden clogs all give the site a cozy air. The orange-colored walls are richly adorned with paintings of Belgian scenes, and what's more, countless beer trademarks tastefully framed. The proprietor is

【Steak Tartar Pure Tenderloin 布鲁塞尔黑椒牛柳】

always glad to talk with anyone interested in the stories behind them.

Specialties

Pot Mussels Cooked in
  Grandmother's Style 原汁海虹
Steak Tartar Pure Tenderloin
  布鲁塞尔黑椒牛柳
Belgian Beef 比利时烩牛肉
Steamed Gray Sole 清蒸龙俐鱼
Holland Maatjes with Mixed Salad
  荷兰鲱鱼
Belgian Blood Sausage 比利时血肠

Goose "N" Duck 鹅和鸭

Restaurant Information

Address: 1st floor, No. 1 Tower of Guanhu Garden (east of Chaoyang Park Overpass), Chaoyang District
（朝阳区朝阳公园桥东侧观湖国际大厦写字楼 1 号楼首层）
Tel: 59283045
Price: average RMB 70 per head
Payment: cash or credit card
Hours: 11:00 am to midnight

The business is open around the clock, playing the dual role of eatery during the day and bar at night. It stages live jazz performance and has such recreational facilities as billiards, darts and shuffleboard. It is a haunt for dart fans, and often hosts tournaments of dart teams.

Specialties

Pies 烤派
Farm Roasted Chicken 农场烤鸡
Hamburgers 汉堡
Salads 沙拉

Brasserie Flo Beijing 福楼

【Fried Codfish with Italian Vinaigrette Pressing 煎鳕鱼柿子椒碎配意大利油醋汁】

【Mushroom Soup with Seafood 海鲜蘑菇汤】

Restaurant Information

Address: 2nd floor of Rainbow Plaza, 16 Third East Ring Road North, Chaoyang District (东三环北路 16 号隆博广场 2 层)

Tel: 65955139

Price: average RMB 160 per head, RMB 88 each for set lunch, RMB 138 for set dinner

Payment: cash or credit card

Hours: 11:00 am to 3:00 pm; 6:00-10:30 pm

In France a "brasserie" implies that the customers are not expected to be formally dressed as in a "restaurant." Brasserie Flo appeals to me due to its casual layout, lively ambience and warm service. It offers set meals with red wine and coffee at fair prices, as part of its efforts to promote French cuisine in the Chinese capital. Each dish boasts fresh ingredients and true French seasonings elaborately prepared by French master hands. The buttery Foie Gras, savory escargots, Normandy clams and tongue-biting desserts all well define the world reputation of French culinary arts. And a glass of French wine in the spacious balcony on a fair-weather day will heighten the unforgettable experience to its peak.

Specialties

Fried Codfish with Italian Vinaigrette Pressing 煎鳕鱼柿子椒碎配意大利油醋汁

Mushroom Soup with Seafood 海鲜蘑菇汤

Fauchon 馥颂

Restaurant Information

Address: Building B1-2, Shi Kong Place, 87 Jianguo Road, Chaoyang District (朝阳区建国路 87 号新光天地 B1-2 楼)
Tel: 65331266
Price: average RMB 200 per head
Payment: cash or credit card
Hours: 10:00 am - 10:00 pm

Fauchon, a luxury restaurant with a history of over 120 years, reflects French gourmet culture. Delicate tastes, superior quality, exceptional innovation along with fresh understanding of food, comfortable living and fine aesthetics are the goals that Fauchon aspires to.

Walk into Fauchon, and your eyes will immediately absorb a feast of colors: the flamboyance of pink, the mystery of black, the feel of fine silver, and the magnificence of gold, yet none giving a sense of ostentation.

Then on the floor below the first you will find a lavish delicatessen, decorated mainly with peach tones, offering specialties such as caviar, smoked trout and foie gras, as well as prepared food, fruits, candies, and cakes.

On the first floor is a patisserie selling French-style breads and coffees, with its gold-themed space divided into eat-in and take-out areas. The bakery offers traditional as well as innovative styles of bread, including crusty butter bread, Madelaine cake, salads, sandwiches, and fresh fruit juices.

The second-floor restaurant, small yet striking with its silver and peach decor, provides specialty French cuisine: foie gras, roast perch, baked tuna steak...

If you are fond of French gourmet cuisine, why not visit Fauchon to experience the romance and beauty of French culture as well as the elegance and passion of French people?

Specialties

Vanilla Layer Cake 香草千层糕

Chocolates 巧克力

Foie Gras 无花果肥鹅肝

Roasted Whole Perch 带皮烤鲈鱼

Suckling Pork Chop 生机乳猪排

Baked Tuna Steak 鲜烤鲔鱼排

Firstar Parfum 浮士德

Address: 3rd floor, Building 19,
China Central Place, Dawang Road,
Chaoyang District（朝阳区大望路华
贸中心 19 楼 3 层）
Tel: 65305799
Price: average RMB 150 per head
Payment: cash or credit card
Hours: 11:00 am to midnight

【Tiramisu with Exotic Fruit 提拉米苏】

As the second outlet of the Firstar chain in Beijing, the restaurant demonstrates its loyalty to French culinary arts, which stress every detail in the cooking and romance in the eating. The chefs believe that even a dish as ordinary as steak can be extraordinary if prepared with supreme ingredients and conscientiousness.

The theme colors — gold and purple, along with the chic tableware of glass and metal, give the space a gracious yet unpretentious look. And hundreds of types of imported wine are available to suit different orders.

A visit to Firstar Parfum entertains the mouth as well as the soul. French music, red wine and caviar, where Champs-Elysees seems not that far away...

Specialties

Smoked Duck Breast with Goose
 Liver Terrine Walnut-Plum Salad
 熏鸭胸肉配法式鹅肝酱
Grilled Salmon Steak of Beluga
 Caviar 扒三文鱼配鱼子酱
Veal Tenderloin with Vegetables and
 Sage Sauce 秘制小牛里脊配甜虾
Tuna Salad of the Mediterranean
 地中海金枪鱼土豆沙拉
Roman Salad 罗马沙拉
Tiramisu with Exotic Fruit 提拉米苏

【Roman Salad 罗马沙拉】

【Smoked Duck Breast with Goose Liver Terrine Walnut-Plum Salad 熏鸭胸肉配法式鹅肝酱】

【Veal Tenderloin with Vegetables and Sage Sauce 秘制小牛里脊配甜虾】

Der Landgraf 兰特伯爵

Restaurant Information

Address: A2 Pufang Road,
Fangzhuang, Fengtai District,
opposite the Carrefour Supermarket
（丰台区方庄蒲方路甲 2 号）
Tel: 67682664, 67682663
Price: average RMB 150 per head
Payment: cash
Hours: 11:00 am to midnight
Website: www.der-landgraf.com

"Der Landgraf" was an earldom invested by the German king in the 12th century. The bar-restaurant is the first business the Landgraf family opened in China, and is consistent with the style of the brand name.

Bitburger, found exclusively in Der Landgraf, is a real big name, whose draft boasts the highest sales volume in Germany. Customers in groups can try the "One-Meter Beer," which is served in smaller glasses on a one-meter tray or all at once in a five-liter cask.

There is a wide range of sausages, including Cabanossi sausage, Bockwurst, potato sausage and curry sausage. Among them, Frankfurter with Pickled Vegetable and Potato Salad is a classic German entree.

The outdoor beer garden is of distinct European style. The interior is the work of experienced Cologne designers, displaying the fashions from the regions along the Rhine.

The site has three banquet parlors. Schwarm is named after the hometown of the Grimm brothers, and therefore exhibits ten glass paintings themed on the fairytales from the Grimms' book. All photos and pictures in the room are gifts from the city of Schwarm. Cologne Hall is named after the home of Bitburger beer. And Beethoven Hall, with a capacity for 50, is entirely adorned with donations from the Beethoven Museum in Bonn. Among these, the most valuable is a left-handed violin. Another attraction of the room is its hand-painted glass lighting panels on the ceiling.

✑Specialties

Mixed German Sausage with Pickled Cabbage and Mashed Potatoes
什锦香肠盘
Garlic French Stick 蒜香法包
Liver Sausage 自制猪肝酱
Fried Apple Rings in Beer Dough with Vanilla Ice-cream
炸苹果圈配香草冰激凌

【Mixed German Sausage with Pickled Cabbage and Mashed Potatoes 什锦香肠盘】

【Fried Apple Rings in Beer Dough with Vanilla Ice-cream 炸苹果圈配香草冰激凌】

Schindler's Tankstelle

申德勒加油站

Restaurant Information

Address: Room 888, west wing of
Ritan Offices, A15 Guanghua Road,
Chaoyang District（朝阳区光华路甲
15 号日坛商务楼西侧 888 号）
Tel: 85626439
Price: average RMB 120 per head
Payment: cash or credit card
Hours: 11:00 am to midnight

The name "Schindler" became known to the Chinese thanks to the blockbuster film directed by Steven Spielberg, *Schindler's List*. Schindler's Tankstelle has nothing to do with film or the US, but it is among the best places in Beijing to try true Deutsch beer and typical Deutsch food. The taste is as good as the sizes and prices.

The business serves Pils Draft and Einsiedler Dark, air-freighted from Germany. Their thick effervescent head can occupy as much as one fourth of the glass. The taste is slightly bitter, but refreshing.

A gourd, a liquor container of old China, is hung at the business' entrance. It is rather whimsical to think of sucking beer from a plump gourd. With its dim lighting and clay-tiled walls and floors, the space has a quiet rustic appeal. Its private rooms are semi-open recesses of cobblestone walls decked with busts of characters from European mythology. Lamps with round clay covers hang down from the arched ceiling. And flamboyant red tablecloths add a lively touch to the predominantly plain setting.

Specialties

Beer 啤酒

Sausages 香肠

Pig Trotters 烤猪脚

Athena 雅典娜

Restaurant Information

Address: 1 Xiwu Street, Sanlitun, north of the Spanish Embassy（三里屯西五街1号）
Tel: 64646036
Price: RMB 100 per head
Payment: cash, check or credit card
Hours: 11:30 am to 11:00 pm

【Mixed Grill Plate 什锦烧烤盘】

Athena sits in a blue building embowered with lush green. The interior is ruled by blue and white, and emits a distinct Mediterranean air. Warm sunshine fall between the leaves, casting mottled shade on the tables in the patio. Behind the bar, of blue ceramic mosaic, you will find a wealth of nectar-like liquors and a fresco of fascinating Mediterranean scenes. The windows, all down to the floor, are of graceful Mediterranean arches. And the waved ceiling feeds the imagination, as if being embraced by breezes from the Mediterranean Sea.

The menu is heavy with grilled items and seafood. Olive oil, feta cheese and herbs enhance the flavors of fresh meat and fish, to a point that pleasantly exceeds one's expectations.

I was told that Greece was a replica of Heaven installed on Earth by the gods, when they were in a good mood and happy with humankind. It is hard not to believe so when eating in Athena. Amazed by every bite, I feel that every taste bud on my tongue was dancing. Fine food and fine scenery — a great remedy for forgetting one's worldly worries.

【Roast Fish of Greek Style 希腊式特色烤鱼】

Specialties

Baklava 巴克拉娃脆香

Mixed Grill Plate 什锦烧烤盘

Greek Souvlaki 希腊串烧

Greek Salad 希腊沙拉

Green Papaya Salad with Yogurt

Dressing 青瓜酸奶沙拉

【Greek Souvlaki 希腊串烧】

【Greek Salad 希腊沙拉】

RAJ 拉兹印度音乐餐厅

Restaurant Information

Address: 31 Gulou West Street, Dongcheng District（鼓楼西大街 31 号）

Tel: 64011675

Price: average RMB 100 per head

Payment: cash or credit card

Hours: 10:00 am to 11:00 pm

Website: www.raj.com.cn

Indian food is known to be laden with spices, but not all. In the sweltering south the diet is strong and piquant, while that in the north is much milder. The food in the RAJ Music Restaurant is in-between.

Top on its menu are: Papada (a crispy snack), Samosa (curry triangle), Tandoor, Lassi (yogurt drink), and Masala Tea. The authentic Indian curries are a sublime supplement to both rice and the thin dosai.

Located in a 200-year-old courtyard west of the Drum Tower in central Beijing, the restaurant creates a sense of mystery, trademark of Indian culture, with dim lighting and heavy drapes, awe-inspiring murals and Buddhist figurines. When folk music fills the air and Indian performers start their joyous dancing, it is hard to believe the site is in the capital of China.

【Tandoori Murg 印式烤鸡肉】

【Sada Pulao 藏红花烤米饭】

【Beef Shajahani 皇家咖喱牛肉】

Specialties

Sada Pulao 藏红花烤米饭

Tandoori Murg 印式烤鸡肉

Dulfi Tangdi Kebab 香料烤鸡腿

Beef Shajahani 皇家咖喱牛肉

Mutton Rogan Josh 咖喱羊肉

The Tandoor 天都里

Restaurant Information

Address: 1st floor, Zhaolong Hotel, 2 Gongti North Road, Chaoyang District

（工体北路 2 号兆龙饭店 1 层）

Tel: 65972211, 65972299 ext. 2112

Price: average RMB 200 each plus 15 % service charge; RMB 68 each for business lunch

Payment: cash or credit card

Hours: 11:30 am to 2:00pm; 5:30-9:30 pm

【Kesar Kulfi 凯萨 库非】

【Murg Schorba Badami 帝王鸡汤】

Indians are crazy about curry, which is strong in the air of every Indian restaurant. The chefs in the Tandoor are all from India, bringing with them more than 50 authentic Indian dishes, such as Indian-style yogurt and a dazzling variety of grilled dishes and dosai (savory pancakes).

The design of the establishment draws on stories of the Jin-dynasty (AD 265-420) monk Faxian and the Tang-dynasty (618-907) monk Xuanzang's pilgrimages west to Central and South Asia. The giant golden Wheel of Eternity at the entrance symbolizes the opening to a time tunnel. The dining space is walled with mirrors, as if people were expected to conduct self-examination and self-improvement upon seeing their reflections in the glass. Strings of palm-size ceramic characters hang down from the ceiling, each holding a quotation by Faxian or Xuanzang. The routes of the two ancient saints' pilgrimages are marked in maps inlaid on the floor and wall, which illustrate a dozen cities en route, including Beijing and Istanbul. The site's five pavilions of varied styles stand for the cultures of the nations the two Buddhist monks traversed along their way.

There are Indian dancing and singing performances every night in the restaurant. As beautiful Indian young women swivel to the ebullient music, before the Indian savories and confections piled up on the tables, few would believe they are still thousands of miles away from India.

Specialties

Chicken Tikka Masala 马撒拉咖喱鸡
Kesar Kulfi 凯萨 库非
Masala Tea 马赛拉茶
Mughlai Paratha 印度千层饼
Murg Schorba Badami 帝王鸡汤
Pakal Paneer 派拉卡派尼儿

【Masala Tea 马撒拉茶】

Annie's 安妮

Restaurant Information

Address: Western gate of SOHO New Town, 88 Jianguo Road, Chaoyang District（朝阳区建国路 88 号 SOHO 现代城西门）

Tel: 65911931 (delivery available)

Price: average RMB 60-100 per head

Payment: cash

Hours: 11:00 am to 11:00 pm

【Grilled New Zealand Lamb Chops 铁扒新西兰羊排】

The inviting smell of pizza from the stone-surfaced oven in the space gives patrons a warm welcome, and invigorates the appetite. Customers can order the ready-to-serve wood-baked pizza, or even try their hand in the making process. Spaghetti and bread with pesto are both big tastes in small items.

The orange-colored walls, checked tablecloths and soft music create a homey environment. The waiters/waitresses can speak good English. And there are separate smoking and no-smoking zones.

【Annie's Pizza 安妮比萨】

Specialties

Annie's Pizza 安妮比萨

Lasagna with Mushrooms and
  Bolognaise Sauce 意式蘑菇肉酱宽扁面

Crispy Garden Salad 田园沙拉

【Crispy Garden Salad 田园沙拉】

【Spaghetti Bolognaise 意粉】

Assaggi 尝试

【Scallops with Black Ink Sauce 意式带子配墨鱼汁】

【Beef Carpaccio with Mustard 薄牛肉配芥末】

Restaurant Information

Address: 1 North Street,
Xingfusancun, Chaoyang District
（朝阳区幸福三村北街 1 号）
Tel: 84544508
Price: average RMB 150 per head
Payment: cash
Hours: 11:30 am to 2:30 pm; 6:00pm
to 11:30 pm

Located in the foreign embassy district in Sanlitun in eastern Beijing, by a shady boulevard Assaggi stands out with its golden facade and huge skylight. The name is Italian for "to taste," beckoning to every dining hipster like myself.

The two-story building is encased in glass walls riveted to metal frames. Bottles of hundreds of brand names glitter on the shelves in the bar section. The open balcony on the second floor is an ideal place to hide away from the daily hustle and bustle, as the natural view of sunshine on the leaves or stars in a night sky can instill a romantic relish to every cup or glass one enjoys there.

Specialties

Beef Carpaccio with Mustard
薄牛肉配芥末

Scallops with Black Ink Sauce
意式带子配墨鱼汁

Tortellini with Aubergine
意式饺子配菠菜汁

Q's Café 素封

【Broiled Lobster Spaghetti with Italian Dressing 龙虾面】

【Fall in Love Set Dinner 浪漫套餐】

Restaurant Information

Address: 1st floor, Sanquan Apartments, 38 Maizidian, Chaoyang District（朝阳区麦子店 38 号三全公寓 1 层）

Tel: 65086038

Price: average RMB 200 per head

Payment: cash or credit card

Hours: 10:00 am to 10:00 pm

Webiste: www.q-cafe.com.cn

Specialties

Traditional Italian Appetizer Platter
意式传统拼盘

Garlic Bread with Salad
蒜味面包配鹅肝沙拉

Breads and Cakes 面包总汇

Margaret Pizza 玛格丽特比萨

The food is a fusion of Japanese and Italian, and the decor blends the East with the West. Both are superbly accomplished. The space is divided into dining and bakery sections. The former is a capacious site of complementary colors and chic design that stresses romance and intimacy. The latter, stylish and relaxed, is a nice spot to squander a couple of hours, reading a book or chatting with friends while regaling on the fresh pastries and mellow coffee prepared by Japanese masters.

Hatsune　隐泉

Restaurant Information

Address: Tower C, Heqiao Group
Building, 8 Guanghua East Road,
Chaoyang District（光华东路8号和
桥大厦C座）
Tel: 65836830/1, 65813939
Price: average RMB 150 per head
Payment: cash
Hours: 10:30 am to 9:00 pm

【AMY 寿司】

Hatsune has the elegance one expects of a Japanese restaurant. The 3m-high entrance with walnut frame conveys a message of graciousness and sanctuary. The first sight behind the ripple-patterned glass doors is a picture of three colorful fish on the wall. The black-and-gray steps fit perfectly with the landscape-themed wall. This is a milieu that can cool down anyone coming in with an overheated mood.

Japanese cuisine stresses the original flavor of the ingredients. The chef selects from the freshest yields of the season, and is careful not to alter their natural tastes in the cooking process. Equal importance is given to the eating ware and dining environment. A Japanese meal therefore is a treat to the mouth as well as the eyes.

Hatsune is wide applauded for its innovative sushi list. Amy sushi is made of seaweed, together with tuna, inside cooked rice rolls. Compared with conventional sushi, which are bundled with the seaweed outside, it spares people the difficulty of breaking through the tough outer skin, enabling them to genteelly consume it in more than one bite.

Hoe Beef is big chunks of beef served in a hoe-shaped container. The strong taste and volume of meat can challenge those of steak.

【Real Love Sushi Roll 爱情不怕辣】

Specialties

Asian Kelp (Undaria pinnatifida) with Vinegar 醋汁裙带菜

Teriyaki Chicken Bento Box 照烧鸡肉便当

Beijing Sushi Roll 北京卷

Raw Shellfish 生吃生贝

Maguro Kabuki Dream 梦幻什锦生鱼片

Seafood Tea-pot Soup 海鲜茶壶汤

Real Love Sushi Roll 爱情不怕辣

【Seafood Tea-pot Soup 海鲜茶壶汤】

【Beijing Sushi Roll 北京卷】

Jiangtai Wuer 将太无二

Restaurant Information

Address: S-108, Building C, Blue
Castle International Apartments, 3
Xidawang Road, Chaoyang District
(朝阳区西大望路 3 号蓝堡国际公寓 C
座 S-108)
Tel: 85999009
Price: average RMB 100 per head
Payment: cash or credit card
Hours: 10:00 am - 10:00 pm

Specialties

CBD Sushi Rolls CBD 国贸商圈寿司
"Diyu" ("Hades") Hotpot 地狱火锅
Eel Rolls 青龙卷

【Assorted Sushi Fashion Mix 寿司盛宴】

Adopting ingredients from Norway, Japan and Canada, including fish, shrimp and shellfish, this restaurant offers unique culinary delights in seafood: CBD sushi rolls, topped with sliced eel and orange roe, with gleaming green avocado in the middle; color, flavor and aroma arrayed before you, yet combined with well-balanced nutrition, with a craving that grows, then the sudden sense of timeless fulfillment of the senses; a meal accompanied by appealing hot rolls, with the sliced fish fire-sprayed before serving — a source of novelty and wonderful surprise.

The restaurant's decor has an intriguing mixture of gold and metal components, Japanese paintings of beautiful women, a North-American-style bar, and fantastic wine shelves.

Len Len 联联

Restaurant Information

Address: 1st floor, Ziming Tower, 12
Xinzhong Street, Dongcheng District
（东城区新中街乙 12 号紫铭大厦 1 层）
Tel: 64156415
Price: average RMB 150 per head
Payment: cash
Hours: 11:30 am to 10:00 pm

Without a parking lot or conspicuous sign, the minimalist exterior of Len Len belies its sleek modernist interior. A long quiet porch bridges its entrance with the dining space, preparing visitors for excitement and surprises in a soon-to-be-discovered world.

The food is Japanese avantgarde. Stewed Pork with Plum Wine is unconventionally bathed in yogurt, but it tastes delicious. The pork is the streaky kind — each piece having three to four layers, alternated by the lean and the fat, which can easily loosen the grease in the braising process while saving the fiber. White Tunny with Crab Eggs is also highly recommended. The crab eggs burst at the slightest chewing, and the thin fish fillet is meltingly tender.

The house enjoys a high reputation among Japanese living in Beijing. Foreigners constitute the majority of its clientele. The service is efficient yet warm, with most waiters/waitresses speaking good Japanese.

Specialties

Flying Fish-eggs Salad 飞鱼籽沙拉
Sweet Sauce Duck with Pumpkin
    Paste and Buckwheat Noodles
    蜜汁和鸭配南瓜酱荞麦面
Shrimp-stuffed Spring Rolls 虾肉春卷

【Shrimp-stuffed Spring Rolls 虾肉春卷】

Sushi Yotsuba 四叶

Address: By the No. 2 Building, Xinyuan Xili Center Street, Chaoyang District
（朝阳区新源西里中街 2 号楼旁）

Tel: 64671837

Price: Average RMB 150-200 per head

Payment: cash

Hours: 5:00-11:00 pm

The business's name is interpreted as (Four-leaf Clover Sushi) in Chinese. A sprig of clover usually has three leaves; when one bears a rare fourth leaf, it is believed to magically bring good luck to the finder. The four leaves represent happiness, health, love and a good job.

Knowing this, customers often instinctively examine the tiny parterre in the lobby. Its potted plants are changed weekly, keeping alive the blossoms as well as the hopes of discovering something unusual amid them. The venue has seating for only 19 diners, making reservations a wise choice. The limited space, however, has the merit of pulling diners and staff closer together, and has a cozy easy appeal.

The sheer majority of foodstuffs are imported from Japan, so that authentic Japanese flavor is guaranteed. The chefs display their sushi art right in front of the diners, deftly working the stuffed rice rolls into delectable shapes and effortlessly sprinkling just the right dose of seasoning on them. A superb companion with the sushi is the Crab Soya-sauce Soup. Among the Sashimi, the shark assortment is rarely seen elsewhere. The finely textured slippery slices are served with crushed garlic.

Specialties

Yotsuba Sushi Set 寿司套餐青四叶
Yotsuba Sashimi Set 刺身套餐特盛四叶
Tuna Sushi 金枪鱼寿司
Roasted Tunny and Rib 烤金枪鱼排骨
Siberian Crab 西伯利亚蟹
Mustard Cuttlefish 芥末章鱼
Crab Soya-sauce Soup 螃蟹酱汤

【Tuna Sushi 金枪鱼寿司】

【Halfbeak Fish Sushi 针鱼寿司】

Shan Fu 山釜

Restaurant Information

Address: A58 Deshengmen West
Street（德胜门西大街甲 58 号）
Tel: 66180362, 66180310
Price: average RMB 100-200 per head
Payment: cash or credit card
Hours: 11:00 am to 10:00 pm

This swanky restaurant focuses on Hong Kong-style hotpot and Korean grills. It makes marvelous sauces. The one made of sea-buckthorn fruit is somewhat spicy; while those wanting a lighter taste can opt for the *Yiweidaodi* ("same taste through to the end"), whose flavor, as its name implies, does not become diluted throughout the dipping and eating process.

Fish Ball is also a feature of the restaurant. Made of finely minced flesh of cuttlefish from Western Africa, it is said to be able to bounce high when dropped to the floor. The Baby Shark is served as a whole fish, chopped into chunks. Shark flesh is of fine texture, and tastes superb. The Beef Fillet is also worth recommending for its melting tenderness.

Specialties

Supreme-grade Beef 上品肥牛
Cuttlefish Balls 鱼丸
Tender Beef Loin 牛里肌

【Supreme-grade Beef 上品肥牛】

【Tender Beef Loin 牛里肌】

Sorabol 萨拉伯尔

Restaurant Information

Address: 3 Jinyu Lane, Wangfujing Street, Dongcheng District （东城区王府井大街金鱼胡同 3 号）
Tel: 65128833 ext. 5711
Price: average RMB 150 per head
Payment: cash, check or credit card
Hours: 11:00 am to 2:00 pm; 6:00-9:00 pm

Sorabol offers more than 30 Korean dishes. One of the must-try items is Hotpot Noodles. Another is Korean-style Grilled Beef Ribs. The top-grade beef ribs are neatly placed around a Korean barbeque stove. When the blood has drained and the meat turned golden, turn the chops over to grill the other side.

After the other side is done, use the scissors to remove the bone and cut the meat into inch-wide slices. Then wrap them, together with shredded shallot, capsicum, garlic and soybean paste, in a piece of lettuce. Now it is ready for a great bite.

In summer the restaurant offers free snacks, such as cold cream, red bean pudding and green bean pudding. In winter and autumn it adds to its menu nourishing Korean Spiced Pig Trotters, Ginseng and Black-bone Chicken Soup, and Ginseng Oxtail Soup.

The site is in a distinct Korean style, as can be seen in the classic Korean furniture, ink paintings, lamps and screens of traditional Korean designs, attendants' uniform as well as the style of service.

Specialties

Grilled Beef Ribs 烤牛排骨
Smoked Beef Tenderloin 熏牛里脊
Hotpot Beef Noodles 牛肉火锅面

Shoufucheng 寿福城

Restaurant Information

Address: B1, Tower A, Cofco Plaza, 8
Jianguomen Street, Dongcheng
District（东城区建国门大街8号中粮
广场A座B1层）
Tel: 65260588
Price: average RMB 150 per head
Payment: cash or credit card
Hours: 10:30 am to 2:00 pm; 5:30-
10:00 pm

Korean cuisine can be summarized as "five colors and five flavors," referring to the colors of red, white, black, green and yellow and the respective tastes of bitter, sweet, sour, hot and salty. This is believed to be good for a long and healthy life, and is at the core of Korean cooking. And no Korean meal can be without garlic, chili or pickled vegetables.

Shoufucheng is the forerunner of Korean gastronomy in Beijing. I love its grills, particularly the beef steaks. The succulent short ribs sizzle the moment they hit the grill iron, but the heat only concentrates its sweetish/salty flavor.

Shoufucheng is among the top-rated Korean restaurants in Beijing. The decor is imperial, with each private room in a different style. The wine stand is of an unusually round shape of multiple layers. Both the wine glasses and crystal glasses are for sale.

【Grilled Beef Fillet 烤生牛里脊】

Specialties

Grilled Beef Steak 烤牛排

Grilled LA Ribs 烤 LA 排骨

Grilled Beef Fillet 烤生牛里脊

Grilled Ox Tripe 烤牛肚

【Stewed Beef Steak in Pot 香瓷纯牛排】

【Grilled Ox Tripe 烤牛肚】

Nina 妮妮娅

Address: 252 Chengfu Road, Haidian District（海淀区成府路 252 号）

Tel: 62656588

Price: average RMB 80 per head

Payment: cash or credit card

Hours: 11:00 am to 2:00 pm, 5:30-10:00 pm

【Fajatas 大虾法嘿塔】

【Nina Corn Flakes 妮妮娅至尊玉米片】

The stylish site is typical Tex-Mex. The sight of sombreros, cactus and other Mexican symbols corresponds with the romantic Latin music in the air. Texan guitarists perform on the diminutive stage every weekend. And during the breaks, customers can flip through the owner's collection of secondhand foreign novels.

Mexico is one of the cradles of chili peppers on Earth, and grows half the known species. The nation boasts more than 140 seasonings with chili. The pungent flavor is so loved by locals that many consume chilies even with fruits.

Pulque is a must in the Mexican diet. After gulping down crispy quesadilla and tacos

【Mexican Delicacies 墨西哥菜集锦】

stuffed with shredded chicken or beef and dipped in salt and paprika, you need a cup of pulque to alleviate the sting on your tongue, giving a final twirl to your Mexican experience.

Specialties

Fajatas 大虾法嘿塔

Nina Corn Flakes 焗海洋玉米饼

Roasted Beef Tenderloin 墨西哥烤牛柳

Flautas 墨西哥炸肉卷

Mexican Taco 墨西哥塔可

【Mexican Taco 墨西哥塔可】

【Flautas 墨西哥炸肉卷】

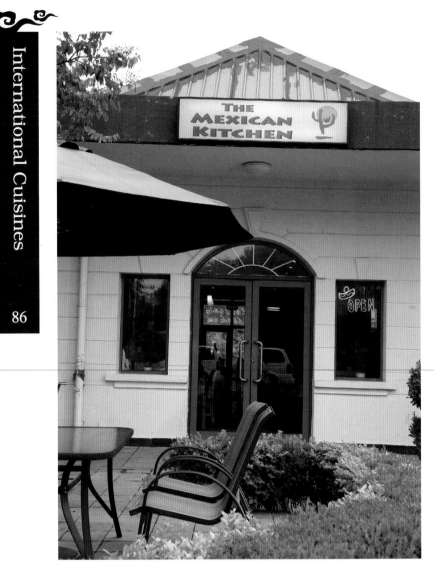

Mexican Kitchen 墨西哥厨房

Restaurant Information

Address: Pinnacle Square, Tianzhu Real Estate Development Zone, Shunyi

District (顺义区天竺房地产开发区日祥广场内)

Tel: 80464558   Price: average RMB 150 per head

Payment: cash   Hours: 10:30 am - 11:00 pm

Traditional Mexican food chiefly includes corn, beans and peppers, as the "three key foods" inevitably served at ordinary family tables. Mexican cuisine is known for its colorful display, intense flavors and variety of spices and sauces. Nearly all the unique sauces are concocted from peppers and tomatoes. Only these specially made sauces can guarantee the purity of taste.

Most of the spices are introduced from the southern United States, while the sauces are concocted by the top chefs. Salsa is the sauce most popular with the customers.

Tacos, using rolled maize tortillas, remain so popular in Mexico that it is sometimes regarded as the archetypal Mexican dish (even KFC restaurants in China offer chicken tacos). Though their taste has been formulated to suit Chinese customers, the chicken tacos still adopt the basic form of a rolled tortilla with delicious fillings, similar to the original Mexican versions.

Making a taco is not complicated: first, put a proper amount of filling such as baked pork, beef or chicken cubes on a palm-sized tortilla; then, add some caraway, onions or varied pepper sauces, according to personal taste; and finally, the tortilla is folded over into a U-shape. Sometimes, kidney beans, mashed potatoes or marinated cactuses leaves are added to the taco, making it even tastier. Tacos have a number of advantages: being convenient to eat, reasonably priced and fully nourishing, as well as being quite delicious. The taco is a type of unrefined staple rich in fiber and vitamin B; while the fillings containing meat, peppers and vegetables can guarantee daily protein, fiber and vitamin needs.

Specialties

Multilayer Corn Nachos with Melted Cheese 多层玉米片及熔化的奶酪

Pan-fried Meat 铁板肉

Mexican Corn Nachos with Tomato Sauce 墨西哥玉米片配西红柿汁

【Mexican Corn Nachos with Tomato Sauce 墨西哥玉米片配西红柿汁】

Elephant 大笨象

Restaurant Information

Address: B1, Huangsheng Tower, 12
Yabaolu Road, Chaoyang District
（朝阳区雅宝路 12 号华声大厦 B1 层）
Tel: 51206538
Payment: cash
Price: average RMB 80 per head
Hours: 11:00 am to 11:30 pm
Website: www.bjelephant.com/
home/company/info.aspx

Elephant is a catering-entertainment establishment. The decor blends traditional and modern elements, with utmost attention to comfort and taste. The site is popular among foreign expats in the business district where it is located. Some Russians visit it four or five times a day, for afternoon tea or a chat over drinks

【Tunny Salad 金枪鱼沙拉】

【Crimson Snapper Eggs 红鱼籽】

with friends.

Customers can opt for buffet (lunch) or order from the extensive 200-dishes menu. Nothing will fall short of your expectations.

Specialties

Elephant Pork Sandwich 大象猪肉包

Russian-style Mixed Grill 俄式烤杂拌

Borsch Soup 红菜汤

Crimson Snapper Eggs 红鱼籽

Kiev Chicken Roll 基辅鸡卷

Fried Pork Chop with Cheese
　计司炸猪排

Tunny Salad 金枪鱼沙拉

Cream Soup 奶油汤

Fried Salmon 香煎鳟鱼

【Russian-style Mixed Grill 俄式烤杂拌】

【Cream Soup 奶油汤】

【Elephant Pork Sandwich 大象猪肉包】

【Kiev Chicken Roll 基辅鸡卷】

Moscow Restaurant 莫斯科餐厅

Restaurant Information

Address: 135 Xizhimenwai Street,
Xicheng District（西直门外大街135号）
Price: average RMB 200 per head
Payment: cash
Hours: 11:00 am to 2:00 pm,
5:00-9:00 pm

【Chicken Salad 首都沙拉】

【Red Caviar with Onion 红鱼籽带洋葱末】

Opened in 1954, the Moscow Restaurant was for a long period among Beijing's top upscale eating venues, and is fondly called "Laomo" ("old Mo") by locals.

The signature courses include Chicken Salad, Moscow Baked Fish in Cream Sauce, and Grilled Steak. Frying, stewing and braising are commonly used, true to the Eastern European diet.

Located in the buzzing Beijing Exhibition Hall plaza establishment, this massive lavishly carved structure displays distinct Slavonic style. Its four copper columns with stately relief are without peer in the Chinese capital. The combination of dignified environment, classical music and savory Russian fare promises an unforgettable experience.

【Fillet Steak in Casserole 罐焖牛柳】

Specialties

Borsch Soup of Moscow 莫斯科红菜汤

Moscow Baked Fish in Cream Sauce
莫斯科式奶油烤鱼

Chicken Salad 首都沙拉

Fillet Steak in Casserole 罐焖牛柳

Breaded Chicken Roll with Kiev
Butter Stuffing 基辅式黄油鸡卷

Red Caviar with Onion
红鱼籽带洋葱末

【Borsch Soup of Moscow 莫斯科红菜汤】

【Moscow Baked Fish in Cream Sauce
莫斯科式奶油烤鱼】

【Breaded Chicken Roll with Kiev Butter Stuffing
基辅式黄油鸡卷】

Petersburg Restaurant

彼得堡餐厅

Restaurant Information

Address: Building 5, 10
Dongzhimennei Avenue, Dongcheng
District（东直门内大街 5 栋 10 号）
Tel: 84078158
Price: average RMB 80-100 per head
Payment: cash
Hours: 10:00 am to 11:30 pm

The food is of traditional style, as is the decor. Invigorating red, yellow and green are the keynote colors. And the opulent paintings themed on Russian folklore nicely convey the spirit of the place.

Borsch Soup, Chicken Salad, Kiev Chicken Roll and Russian-style Stewed Beef are big names in Russian cuisine that well deserve their delicious reputation. Kisel (fruit drink) and Kvas (light beer) are two impressive indigenous Russian beverages. And every plate and glass is brought to the table with contagious Russian hospitality.

【Stew Mutton 炖羊肉】

Specialties

Cheese Beefsteak 奶酪牛排

Pork Fillet Served with Wine Sauce

红酒猪肉

Assorted Russian Salami Plate

萨拉米肠

Stew Mutton 炖羊肉

Salmon Roast with Vegetables

蔬菜煎三文鱼

Stuffed Trout Jelly 馅虹鳟鱼冻

【Stuffed Trout Jelly 馅虹鳟鱼冻】

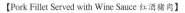

【Pork Fillet Served with Wine Sauce 红酒猪肉】

【Assorted Russian Salami Plate 萨拉米肠】

【Salmon Roast with Vegetables 蔬菜煎三文鱼】

【Cheese Beefsteak 奶酪牛排】

Chenfuji 陈福记

Restaurant Information

Address: 2nd floor, Winterless Center, Tower A, 1 West Dawang Road,

Chaoyang District (朝阳区西大望路1号温特莱中心A座2层)　　Tel: 65388456

Price: average RMB 80 per head, RMB 48 to 60 each for business lunch for four

Payment: cash or credit card　　　　　　　　Hours: 11:30 am to 10:00 pm

【Imperial Golden Fried Rice 金镶银炒饭】

【Coffee Almond Ribs 咖啡杏仁排骨】

Chenfuji has been working on its select Cantonese and Singaporean menu during its history of more than 50 years. Its signature item is Imperial Golden Fried Rice, a mixture of rice, crab flesh and shrimp in a tantalizing golden color. To ensure the distinct flavors, chefs use only rice harvested the previous year and cooked the previous day and the freshest crabmeat. Among the condiments are the "four treasures of kitchen" — green shallots, old ginger, onion and garlic. After being finely stir-fried for 15 to 20 minutes, every grain of rice shines with a golden egg coating, making every mouth at the table water. Coffee Almond Ribs and Three Cups Chicken with Shaoxing Rice Wine are also worthy recommendations. Chenfuji does a great job in blending styles of the East and West, while preserving its own uniqueness. The vanilla-tinged Bah Kut Tea goes surprisingly well with fried bread strips.

Specialties

Imperial Golden Fried Rice
金镶银炒饭
Coffee Almond Ribs 咖啡杏仁排骨
Black Pepper Crabs 黑椒螃蟹
Mango Pudding 芒果布丁

【Black Pepper Crabs 黑椒螃蟹】

Alameda 茵茵

Restaurant Information

Address: Beili, Sanlitun North Street,
Chaoyang District（朝阳区三里屯北
街北里）

Tel: 62186060, 64178084

Price: average RMB 50-100 per head

Payment: cash

Hours: 10:00 am to 10:30 pm

The Brazilian restaurant serves authentic South American dishes. Its owner and leading chef are both Brazilians. And most patrons are from South America. From Monday to Friday the restaurant offers a set business lunch for RMB 60 that comes with a free bread platter.

Feijoada (brewed meat with beans) is considered a national delicacy of Brazil, and is a regular accompaniment for weekend nights when locals watch their favorite sport — football — on TV. In the bar section, the most prominent item is Cachaca, a strong liquor popular among Brazilians. The annual per capita consumption averages 11 liters. Guarana is a soda energy drink. It is the designated beverage for the national football league of Brazil, and is referred to as one of the "three treasures of the nation," the other two being football and the Cha Cha.

Specialties

Feijoada 豆子炖肉
Brazilian Rum 巴西黑豆饭
Codfish with Asparagus 银鳕鱼
Chocolate Tart 巧克力塔
Green Salad 田园沙拉

【Chief Salad 首长沙拉】

【Green Salad 田园沙拉】

【Chocolate Tart 巧克力塔】

【Codfish with Asparagus 银鳕鱼】

Garden of Delights 饕餮源

【Fish Slices with "Three Fresh Ingredients" 三鲜生鱼片】

【Grilled Beef·with Pineapple牛肉配菠萝烧烤】

Restaurant Information

Address: 53 Dong'anmen Street, Dongcheng District (东城区东安门大街 53 号)

Tel: 51385688

Price: average RMB 300-500 per head

Payment: cash or credit card

Hours: 12:00 am to 2:00 pm and 6:00-11:00 pm, from Monday to Friday; 6:00-11:00 pm on weekends

Website: www.gardenofdelights.com.cn/index.asp

The establishment borrows its name from *Garden of Earthly Delights*, the center panel of a famous triptych by Dutch painter Hieronymus Bosch. Inspired by this magnificent work, the proprietor selected the section on worldly pleasures for the theme of the restaurant, which is repeated in the logo, facade, lighting boxes, menus and a mural, as a salute to humanity.

The Venezuelan chef introduces elements of French cuisine into South American food, giving it an elegant touch and unique relish.

Light blue and brown dominate the site. Golden sunshine pours down through the vaulted ceiling, bathing the Renaissance paintings on the yellow-brick walls and leafy tropical plants to the side. Ethereal music floats through the air, creating a charm of peace and ease.

Specialties

Grilled Beef with Pineapple 牛肉配菠萝烧烤

Fish Slices with "Three Fresh Ingredients" 三鲜生鱼片

Mare 古老海

【Sizzling Garlic Prawns 蒜味橄榄油烫虾仁】

【Chicken Croquettes 脆炸鸡肉卷】

Restaurant Information

Address: Xingfu Ercun, 14 Xindong Road, Chaoyang District（朝阳区新东路14号幸福二村）

Tel: 64165431, 64171456

Price: average RMB 150

Hours: 10:00 am to 2:00 pm, 5:30 pm to midnight (orders accepted before 10:30 pm)

The frills-free gray facade of the Mare restaurant can be easily overlooked by less-than-attentive eyes. "Mare" (pronounced ma-ray) is the old Latin word for sea, the main attraction of the Spanish landscape and the source of many ingredients in the Spanish diet.

The restaurant's intention is to serve traditional Spanish flavors. Most dishes are seasoned with wholesome olive oil. Wine is es-sential in Spanish meals. Many Spaniards have five meals every day. Long hours are spent at the table, eating and chatting. When the last meal finally concludes at midnight, some will slip into a bar to enjoy one more glass. "No time for sleep?" and they reply: "We will have plenty when settling in the grave."

Specialties

Paella 西班牙肉菜饭

Chicken Croquettes 脆炸鸡肉卷

Sizzling Garlic Prawns

蒜味橄榄油烫虾仁

Tapas 达帕世

Restaurant Information

Address: Sanlitun North Street, Chaoyang District, opposite of the Industrial and Commercial Bank of China (三里屯北街工商银行对面)
Tel: 64178038 ext. 7946
Price: RMB 150 per head
Hours: 10:30 am to midnight
Website: www.tapas.com.cn

【Seafood Paella 海鲜饭】

Mr. Carlos Chordi is from Spain, where he trained in the most reputed School for Chefs. After a successful career in Paris and Porto, he decided to bring Spanish cuisine to China, and opened the first Spanish restaurant in Beijing, Tapas, in 1998.

"Tapas" refers to a variety of Spanish appetizers, which first appeared in Andalusia in the 19th century. To keep flies out of cups, bar tenders often put a plate or other flat things on the drinks they served; later bread became an alternative cover. Some people were then inspired to top it with a piece of cheese, bacon or a few olives, and make it into a snack.

Tapas has a beautiful setting decorated with Spanish ornaments. It provides the most typical and exquisite Spanish Rice (Paella), Spanish Omelets, Spanish Tomato and Garlic Bread and so many other delicacies, which can accompany their delicious Spanish wines.

The strong savory Seafood Paella is rice, which is fried, boiled and then roasted, with a good assortment of side ingredients, including chicken, squid, shrimp, scallop, onion, tomato, pepper and lemon. The two-person serving is of a gener-ous size. The Egg and Potato Tortilla is a traditional Tapas, and is loved for its light taste.

The restaurant logo is a fighting bull against a flaming red background. There are a good many bright-colored posters of Spanish themes, such as bulls, Flamingo dancing and revelry over Spanish spirits. Vibrant Latin music resonates through the space, filling the imagination with ebullient scenes of Spanish life.

Specialties

Seafood Paella 海鲜饭
Chocolate Cake 巧克力蛋糕
Tomato Soup 西红柿汤
Tapas 土豆鸡蛋饼

Banana Leaf 蕉叶

Address: 4 Gongti North Road behind the Comfort Inn, Chaoyang District（朝阳区工体北路4号院内）
Tel: 65068855, 65063399
Price: average RMB 80 per head
Payment: cash or credit card
Hours: 11:00 am to 11:00 pm

Thai cuisine is known for its unique tart and spicy flavors. The masterpiece of Banana Leaf is the Curry Crab, which excels in its hot/sweet curry sauce that incorporates multiple spices and coconut extracts. It goes particularly well with rice or other staples, such as Thai-style fried rice noodles, Indian pancakes, and the Taro Rice. Before concluding the meal, one should not miss the marvelous desserts, including coconut cake and mango-coconut sticky rice.

The menu designed like a gourmet magazine, which offers information and tips on Thai

【Imperial Thai Shark-fin Pot 泰皇堡仔翅】

food alongside the conventional list of dishes and prices.

The restaurant in Sanlitun is imbued with a relaxed pastoral ambience. The rattan furniture is the same as what can be widely found in Thai homes. The rockery, waterfall and green vines winding across the ceiling all create a refreshing natural scene.

The waiters and waitresses are all clad in traditional Thai costume. They may speak using any cooking utensil at hand as if it were a microphone, beckoning to customers to join the singing and dancing with the band. As the entire room sways with the joyful music, lead by Thai performers, the space becomes ebullient.

Specialties

Curry Crab 咖喱皇炒蟹

Chicken-drumstick Mushrooms (Coprinus comatus) with Abalone Sauce 鲍汁鸡腿菇

Imperial Malay Curry 皇牌马来咖喱

Stone Pot Snowflake Beef 石窝烧雪花牛肉

Imperial Thai Shark-fin Pot 泰皇堡仔翅

Crab Flesh Mixed Fruit Salad 鲜杂果蟹肉沙律

【Stone Pot Snowflake Beef 石窝烧雪花牛肉】

【Crab Flesh Mixed Fruit Salad 鲜杂果蟹肉沙律】

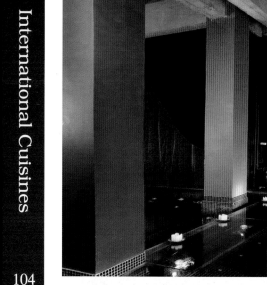

Pink Loft 粉酷

Address: 6 Sanlitun South Road, Chaoyang District（朝阳区三里屯南路6号）
Tel: 62186060
Price: RMB 50-100 per head
Payment: cash or credit card
Hours: 11:00-2:00 am

The Pink Loft is, as you can imagine, completely pink. The pink walls, floors, curtains and gowns of the waitresses in the dim light successfully create a dreamy ambience. It serves modified Southeast Asian courses, with Thai cuisine as center stage. The food is as hot as Thailand's climate and as sweet as its people's smile. Adjacent to the ocean, Thai people have lots of seafood and fresh vegetables in their diet. Tom Yum Soup is particular to Thai restaurants, and cannot be missed. Its sour and piquant flavor comes from green lemon and indigenous Thai pepper. Coconut Milk Fish is slightly hot, and is savory with the fragrance of coconut.

【Papaw Salad 木瓜沙拉】

The setting is gorgeously Thai style, and shows attention to every detail. Concealed in the pink shadows and lulled by the soft Thai music, one unknowingly becomes lost in the relaxing atmosphere. Through the glass floors, customers on the second floor can peek at the crowds downstairs, or admire the lotus lights in the pool below. The private rooms on the third floor are partitioned from others with bead and gauze curtains, and feature high-back Chinese-style chairs. Flame-red lamps hang from the ceiling, investing the whole space with tropical colors.

Specialties

Papaw Salad 木瓜沙拉
Curry Chicken 咖喱鸡
Mango Chicken Fillet 芒果鸡条
Fried Rice with Seafood 海鲜炒饭

【Curry Chicken 咖喱鸡】

【Mango Chicken Fillet 芒果鸡条】

Very Siam 暹罗泰

Restaurant Information

Address: 10A Xinyuan Xili (lane
northwest of Yuyang Hotel)新源西里
东街甲 10 号
Tel: 84510031
Price: RMB 50-100 per head
Payment: cash or credit card
Hours: 11:30 am to 11:30 pm

The site's exterior as well as interior look very Thai. The white edifice is surrounded by coconut trees. A golden sculpture of an elephant, a symbol of good luck, stands by the entrance, extending blessings to every visitor. A Thai goddess statue is posed right behind the door. The 400-square-meter dining space is lavishly decorated with more than 100 works of art that the restaurant owner purchased at steep prices from Thailand, including wood carvings by craftspeople serving the royal family. Even the restrooms are located in a recess by a wardrobe of silverware. Warm sunshine pours down through the magnifying glass ceiling, and shines down into everyone's hearts.

The food is equally lofty. The Steamed Fish with Lemon is impressive, with a heavenly tang to the tender pieces of fish. The Golden Curry Chicken boasts inexpressible flavors mingling curry, coconut milk and other spices. The fanciful Mango Iceberg is made of mango slices, fruit paste and jelly beads on crushed ice. A similarly divine dessert is Burbur Chacha, a classic sweet of Southeast Asia, which includes a variety of fruits chips and crushed ice soaked in condensed milk and coconut juice. It gives a memorable ending to the dining experience, escalating it to a lovely peak.

I am convinced that happiness is a habit. Happiness comes from being conscientiously content and appreciative of life, rather than from the amount of wealth one owns. I feel happy with my gourmet adventures, and will continue them.

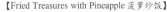

Specialties

Fried Treasures with Pineapple
菠萝炒饭
Seafood Salad 海鲜沙拉
Steamed Fish with Lemon
清蒸柠檬鱼

【Seafood Salad 海鲜沙拉】

【Fried Treasures with Pineapple 菠萝炒饭】

Istanbul　伊斯坦布尔

Address: Behind the Friendship Store,
B7 Xiushui South Street, Chaoyang
District（秀水南街B7号友谊商店后）
Tel: 65032700
Price: average RMB 50-100 per head
Payment: cash
Hours: 10:00 am to midnight

As its name implies, the restaurant offers Turkish fare, which is known for the lengthy and complicated cooking, mostly baking and braising, process. The grills are great, as are their tea, coffee and yogurt, which are genuine Turkish imports. The Turkish coffee is extraordinarily strong, the dregs taking up half of the cup. The Turkish custom is to dump the dregs on a plate after finishing the beverage; it is said the form of the scattered dregs reveals one's future. Turkish tea is boiled over flames. The amber-colored drink tastes similar to spiced black tea.

The decor is entirely Turkish. Impassioned belly dances are staged at dinnertime every Friday and Saturday.

Specialties

Istanbul Salad 伊斯坦布尔特色沙拉

Middle Eastern 1,000-layer Pastry
中东千层饼

Turkish Grilled Perch 土耳其包烤鲈鱼

Turkish Barbeque 土耳其烤肉

Friday's　星期五

Restaurant Information

Address: 1st floor of Huapeng
Towers, 19 Northeast Third Ring
Road North, Chaoyang District（朝
阳区东三环北路 19 号华鹏大厦 1 层）
Tel: 65975314
Price: average RMB 100-150 per head
Payment: cash or credit card
Hours: 11:00 am to midnight

The term "TGIF" — Thank Goodness It's Friday — is the best example of American humor. Friday means people, fazed by the routine work of five days, are suddenly free to drink as much as possible and stay out as late as desired.

The restaurant doesn't have a perplexingly long menu, but mi-

fashioned ceiling fans spin adagio; cute ornaments are scattered around the space, such as sailboat replicas, glassware and old photographs. The waiters/waitresses, with various fashioned caps on their heads and clusters of badges and pendants on their chests, attend to each table with infectious friendliness.

Specialties

Cocktails 鸡尾酒

Barbecued Ribs 烤肋排

Stuffed Potato Skins 炸马铃薯皮

Fried Calamari 炸洋葱圈

Tomato Basil Soup 紫苏番茄汤

Clam Chowder 蛤蜊浓汤

Mocha Mud Pie 摩卡咖啡冰淇淋派

nor adjustments are made every three months. The food comes in large portions, and there are no rules for how things are matched or consumed. Usually a dozen new courses debut every March or April.

The site is imbued with a relaxed and nostalgic air. Painted glass lamps cast a soft light; old-

Alfa　拉米熊

Restaurant Information

Address: 6 Xingfu Yicun, Chaoyang
District（朝阳区幸福一村 6 号）
Tel: 64130085/6
Price: average RMB 80 per head
Payment: cash
Hours: 11:00 am to 11:00 pm

The bar stands out in Beijing's dining circles for presenting the culinary art invented by 17th-century French missionary Rene Lamy. Mr. Lamy was a skilled cook who believed that a conversation about food was one of the best ways to start communication with locals. Whenever he arrived in a new place, he never hurried to advocate his religious beliefs. Instead he studied local cuisine, and won the locals' trust through cooking and sharing meals with them. In this process he blended French gastronomy with those in his host countries in Southeast Asia, and created his exclusive "missionary cuisine." He later detailed this in his *Lamy Cookbook*.

Alfa is loyal to Lamy's book. Most items are steamed or fried, and the ingredients selection and cooking methods are not difficult at all. These characteristics, the result of the limitations of kitchens from a less opulent time,

nevertheless keep intact the original flavors of foods and their nutritional value.

The bar lies in a reclusive lane in the bustling Chaoyang district. The inside is, however, in no way too ascetic. Chic candles, stylish mosaic walls, gurgling water, along with the lively music, all appeal to present-day epicureans.

【Southeast Asian Grilled Beef 东南亚烤牛肉】

【Okinawa Shrimp Balls 冲绳凤梨虾球】

【Chicken Vegetable Puree Soup 鸡丝碧绿汤】

Specialties

Okinawa Shrimp Balls 冲绳凤梨虾球

Chicken Vegetable Puree Soup
鸡丝碧绿汤

Southeast Asian Grilled Beef
东南亚烤牛肉

Nuage 庆云楼

Address: 22 Qianhai Dongyan,
Shichahai, Xicheng District（什刹海
前海东沿 22 号）
Tel: 64019581
Price: average RMB 100 per head
Payment: cash
Hours: 10:00 am to 10:00 pm
Website: www.nuage.com.cn

The name means "cloud" in French, and is true to the venue's transcendent aura. The menu features the cuisine of southern Vietnam, whose inimitable flavors can be best captured in the Papaya Salad, of green papaya with red pepper and minced

【Spring Onion Scallops 葱香扒扇贝】

【Fresh Mint Shrimp Spring Rolls 灯影生春卷】

peanuts.

The decor borrows traditional Chinese elements, but is still distinctly Vietnamese, as revealed by the tableware, ornaments, furniture and music, as well as the staff uniforms. The balcony on the third floor offers views of the centuries-old Drum and Bell towers to the east, Houhai Lake in the west, and the Silver Ingot Bridge below. Watching the flow of people and vehicles below the window, one will cherish even more these rare moments of enjoying a hearty repast in peace and leisure.

Specialties

Cold Rice Noodles with Spring Rolls

凉拌米粉和蔬菜春卷

Fresh Mint Shrimp Spring Rolls

灯影生春卷

Papaya Salad 青木瓜飘香

Spring Onion Scallops 葱香扒扇贝

【Cold Rice Noodles with Spring Rolls
凉拌米粉和蔬菜春卷】

【Papaya Salad 青木瓜飘香】

Famous Chinese Teas

As one of the world's top three beverages (with coffee and cocoa), tea helps relax one's nerves and alleviate both mental and physical stress.

According to different methods in processing, tea is divided into red, green, oolong, yellow, white and black categories.

West Lake Longjing

Acknowledged as the "Queen of Green Tea," West Lake Longjing ("dragon well") tea gets its name from the place that produces it. Its tea leaves, flat and straight, resemble orchid petals in shape, and are either jade green or viridian. They have a bittersweet flavor and an aftertaste resembling the taste of fresh olives.

Huangshan Maofeng

This is a green tea produced in the scenic Huangshan Mountains of Anhui Province. Its leaves are shaped like the tongue of a sparrow, slender and a bit upturned at the edge. The brew is apricot-yellow in color, tastes bittersweet, and has a permeating aroma.

Dongting Biluochun

This is a green tea produced in the Dongting Mountains by Lake Tai. Its rolled-up leaves look like spiral shells and have a color that reminds one of the lush greens of spring, hence its name "bi-luo-chun," or "green-conch-spring." The brew has a wafting gentle fragrance and leaves a pleasant bouquet on the tongue.

Anxi Tieguanyin

This is a high-quality variety of oolong tea produced in Fujian Province. The brew is golden in color and has a pleasant aftertaste. The leaves can be steeped many times.

Dongding Oolong

Honored as the best of Taiwan tea, it grows on Taiwan's Dongding Mountain, hence its name. Its leaves curl up into half-spheres and are dark green in color. The brew is yellowish green and has a fragrance resembling that of sweet-scented osmanthus.

Wuyi Dahongpao

It is a rare variety of oolong tea yielded by a handful of trees that grow out of some rock crevices on Wuyi Mountain in Fujian Province. Due to its rarity, the tea is very expensive.

Junshan Yinzhen

It is a yellow tea produced on Junshan Island in Dongting Lake, in Hunan Province. It gets its name from its native place as well as the shape of its leaves, which look like silver needles, or "yinzhen" in Chinese.

Baihao Yinzhen

This is a white tea produced in Fujian Province. The brew is white in color. Since the fresh leaves are sun-dried, without being baked or rubbed, their white dusting remains intact after they become dry. White tea helps strengthen the body's resistance against viruses.

Qimen Red

This is a high-quality red tea produced around Qimen County in Anhui Province. The brown brew is very refreshing and aromatic.

Yunnan Pu'er

This is produced around Yunnan's Xishuangbanna and refers to brick tea of any variety that is processed through steaming and compressing. Pu'er is valued not only for its fragrance and flavor, but also its medicinal effect. It helps reduce obesity and high cholesterol, strengthen the stomach, as well as improve sleep.

Choice Restaurants

Every May and October the brasserie sets up festooned tents in the eastern garden, and hosts parties with performances by Bavarian bands. The merry scene will remind people of the streets of Munich.

21st Floor Restaurant
二十一层餐厅

Restaurant Information

Address: The 21st floor of the Great Wall Sheraton Hotel, 10 East Third Ring Road North, Chaoyang District (朝阳区东三环北路10号长城饭店21层)

Tel: 65905566 ext. 2202 or 2295

Price: average RMB 200 per head, plus 15% service charge

Payment: cash or credit card

Hours: 11:30 am to 2:00 pm; 5:30-10:00 pm

True to its name, the restaurant is perched on the 21st floor of the five-star hotel, overlooking the upscale embassy district below. The food is of Sichuan and Cantonese cuisines, emphasizing wholesomeness without compromising on taste.

The site, dominated by gold and black, evokes the charm of traditional Chinese culture. Calligraphies of Chinese poems are ubiquitous in the space, even on the carpet, chair backs, lampshades and uniforms, as well as the walls.

The most eye-catching items in the restaurant are the line of 19 ink paintings of street scenes of old Beijing, which add nostalgic sentiments to the site and a humanistic touch to the aristocratic decor. The tableware ingeniously mingles Chinese characters with post-modernist colors. And the waitress' uniforms, gold and black *qipao*, or cheongsams, are also printed with ancient Chinese poems, to effectively enhance the graceful ambience of the setting.

【Bird's Nest in Papaya 木瓜官燕】

Specialties

Prawns with White Chili 白辣椒炒虾球

Abalone with Sea Cucumber

鲍汁灵芝菇海参

Bifengtang Crab 避风塘雪蟹

Fotiaoqiang 佛跳墙

(steamed abalone with shark's fin

and fish maw in broth)

Bird's Nest in Papaya 木瓜官燕

Dimsum Shrimp Dumplings

水晶虾饺王

【Abalone with
Sea Cucumber
鲍汁灵芝菇海参】

【Bifengtang Crab 避风塘雪蟹】

【Fotiaoqiang 佛跳墙】

【Prawns with White Chili 白辣椒炒虾球】

Brazilian Churrascos

巴西烤肉餐厅

Restaurant Information

Address: 1st floor, Crowne Plaza
Parkview Hotel, 8 North Fourth Ring
Road Center, Chaoyang District（朝
阳区北四环中路 8 号五洲皇冠假日酒
店 1 层）
Tel: 84982288 ext. 6178
Price: RMB 98 for lunch buffet, RMB
138 for dinner buffet, plus 15%
service charge
Payment: cash or credit card
Hours: 11:30 am to 2: 30 pm; 5:30-
10:30 pm

Specialties

Brazilian Grill 巴西烤肉

Copacabana Surf 柯巴卡巴纳风味

【Copacabana Surf 柯巴卡巴纳风味】

The restaurant is a site of fascinating ambience, hot music and the finest grills.

The dazzling variety of grills is marinated with a secret sauce before being moved to low flames in the open kitchen. The meat and sausages can be paired with different soups, salads and desserts, and also should not remain unaccompanied by something from the restaurant's long cocktail list.

【Brazilian Grill 巴西烤肉】

Café Cha 香格里拉咖啡

Restaurant Information

Address: 1st Floor, Shangri-La Hotel, 29 Zizhuyuan Road, Haidian District（海淀区紫竹院路 29 号香格里拉饭店 1 层）

Tel: 68412211 ext. 2715

Price: Breakfast (daily) at RMB 158 per head, Supper at RMB 338 (Mon. & Sat.) and RMB 298 (other days), Lunch at RMB 298 (Sat.), RMB 338 (Sun.), and RMB 428 with free champagne (Sun.), Above prices do not include 15% service charge.

Payment: cash or credit card

Hours: 6:00 to midnight

Shangri-La is a paradise hidden in the mountains of Tibet, as described by James Hilton in his novel *Lost Horizon*, where people can feel a peace of mind and soul. Café Cha carefully designed a landscaped garden in a Chinese courtyard style to create a cozy and pleasant atmosphere.

Café Cha's open kitchen and on-the-spot cooking buffets provide a full display of fresh ingredients, with authentic dishes and desserts representing different culinary styles of the world. Such an arrangement creates its own sensatory paradise. The beautiful and individualized tableware reveals the designer's respect for gastronomy. The international buffet served throughout the day at Café Cha includes delicacies from a range of countries, including Italian and Indian dishes, Japanese sushi, Beijing Duck, and a wide choice of fresh seafood and desserts.

Specialties

Pizza 比萨

spaghetti 意大利面

Indian curry 印度咖喱

Japanese sushi 日本寿司

sashimi 生鱼片

desserts 甜品

Café Swiss 瑞士咖啡厅

Restaurant Information

Address: 1st Floor, Beijing Hongkong Macau Center Swissotel, 2 Chaoyangmen North Street, Dongcheng District（东城区朝阳门北大街 2 号港澳中心瑞士酒店 1 层）
Tel: 65532288 ext. 2127
Price: RMB 100, plus 15% service charge
Payment: cash or credit card
Hours: 8:00 am to 9:00 pm

Beijing Hongkong Macau Center Swissotel is a five-star hotel located in Beijing's business center on the Second Ring Road East. It is surrounded by commercial buildings and foreign embassies. Café Swiss, reviewed as the "best star-rated hotel restaurant" in Beijing, has a bright and ingenious design with an open kitchen. A wide choice of famous Swiss chocolate desserts and cakes are its specialties.

The heartening Swiss cheese fondue (hotpot) and roasted cheese are winter gourmet items that one cannot miss at the Café Swiss. The yellow glow of the mellow fondue soup and its permeating fragrance are simply irresistible. Diners should remember that they should not have cold drinks with the fondue, or it may cause indigestion.

Café Swiss is a pleasant experience for cheese lovers, where they can have authentic Swiss cheese and cakes, in the midst of a gourmet Swiss ambience.

Specialties

Nut Cake 干果蛋糕

Strawberry and Chocolate Cake 草莓巧克力蛋糕

Green Tea Cake 绿茶蛋糕

Mango and Yoghurt Cake 芒果酸奶蛋糕

Cuisine Gallery 凯涛餐厅

The restaurant serves both classic dishes from France as well as from Asian countries, including China. A gem on its menu is Terrine of Goose Liver with Beer, Caramelized Onion Sauce and Toast. The incumbent chief chef is passionate about giving expression to his experience from multiple countries in his creation of new dishes, and never tires of surprising and tantalizing his customers.

The posh decor, a masterwork by French designer Philippe Ollendorff, works well with the dim lighting and low music, to create an intoxicating romantic ambience.

Restaurant Information

Address: 2nd floor, Novotel Xinqiao Beijing Hotel, 2 Dongjiaominxiang, Dongcheng District, northwest exit of Chongwenmen subway station
（东城区东交民巷 2 号北京新侨诺富特饭店 2 层）
Tel: 65133366 ext. 2206
Price: average RMB 180 per head, plus 15% service charge
Payment: cash or credit card
Hours: 11:30 am to 2:00 pm; 5:30-9:30 pm

Specialties

Terrine of Goose Liver with Beer
秘制鹅肝批配啤酒
Caramelized Onion Sauce and Toast
洋葱甜酱和烤面包

【Caramelized Onion Sauce and Toast 洋葱甜酱和烤面包】

Danieli's Restaurant
丹尼艾丽斯意大利餐厅

Restaurant Information

Address: 2nd floor, St. Regis Hotel
Beijing, 21 Jianguomenwai Street,
Chaoyang District （朝阳区建国门外
大街 21 号国际俱乐部饭店 2 层）
Tel: 64606688, 62186060
Price: average RMB 500, plus 15%
service charge
Payment: cash or credit card
Hours: 9:30 am to 10:00 pm

Italy is dubbed the mother of European cuisine. Italian food has its roots in the imperial court of the Roman Empire and Fiorentina of the Renaissance era. Wheat and pasta items are its strong point.

Danieli's has a wide variety of classic Italian courses, and is the best choice in Beijing for fresh truffles. Its truffles are imported from the Piemonte region. And it serves rare white truffles every

December. The leading chef is a master hand of northern Italian cuisine, which features thick delicious sauces with the dishes.

The decor is of an elaborate Renaissance style, with gold being the theme color. Splendid designs and handmade wall paintings dazzle around the columns and walls under the lofty vaulted ceiling. Ceramic platters, glass wares and giant pendant lamps remind one of the heydays of Florence.

Take a seat in one of the classic-fashioned armchairs, and indulge yourself on authentic Italian fare and wine, it is an experience you will never forget.

Specialties

Steak and Foie Gras Sauce
牛排和鹅肝酱

Linguine with Lobster 龙虾意面

129

Horizon Chinese Restaurant

海天阁

Restaurant Information

Address: 1st floor, Kerry Center Hotel, 1 Guanghua Road, Chaoyang District
（朝阳区光华路1号香格里拉北京嘉里中心饭店1层）
Tel: 65618833-41
Price: average RMB 300 per head, plus 15% service charge
Payment: cash or credit card
Hours: 10:30 am to 2:30 pm; 5:30-10:00 pm

The Kerry Center Hotel, of the Shangri-la Group, is a stylish construction that smoothly blends eastern and western architectural elements.

The food is Cantonese style. Seafood lovers will be enchanted by its buffet lunch, which uses shrimp, all plump and fresh, in half of the abundant choices. The Fish Maw Soup is far from run of the mill. And the Tortoise and Herb Jelly as well as the Mango Pudding are marvelous. Discounts are available on the weekend.

Specialties

Gold-foil Imperial Shark's Fin

金箔宫廷大排翅

Gold-foil Imperial Bird's Nest

金箔宫廷成牙官燕

Shaozhou-style Iced Sea Crab

潮式原汁冻花蟹

Crab Meat, Bamboo Fungus and

Tofu Clay-pot 蟹黄竹笙玉脂豆腐煲

Crispy Wheat-flavored Shrimp

生煎脆口麦香虾

Jaan Restaurant 加安法餐

【Lobster Soup with Onion
加安泡沫龙虾汤配香葱螃蟹饼】

【Cariban Chocolate with Vanilla Ice Cream
加勒比巧克力天妇罗配波本香草冰淇淋】

Restaurant Information

Address: 1st floor of the main building of Raffles Beijing Hotel, 33 East Chang'an Avenue, Dongcheng District （东长安街 33 号北京饭店莱佛士酒店主楼 1 层）
Tel: 65263388 ext. 4186
Price: average RMB 300 per head, plus 15% service charge
Payment: cash or credit card
Hours: 12:00 am to 2:00 pm; 6:30-10:00 pm

Specialties

Foie Gras with Asparagus 鹅肝芦笋酱

Sauteed Sea Fish with Tomato
煎海舫鱼配油浸番茄

Lobster Soup with Onion
加安泡沫龙虾汤配香葱螃蟹饼

Raffles is a forerunner in the international hotel industry, and is listed among the top 25 hotels in Asia. Raffles Beijing is the company's first outlet in China.

Jaan is an intimate yet sumptuous dining place in the hotel. The food features modern French cuisine enriched with delicate eastern flavors and aromas, all created from the season's finest ingredients. Lines of top-grade French wines peek out over the bar, enticing the diners.

The decor epitomizes French grace. And the centerpiece of the restaurant is the stunning 1924 original dance floor, on which sits a historic grand piano.

Kempinski-Paulaner

凯宾斯基啤酒坊

Restaurant Information

Address: Ground floor, Kempinski
Hotel, 50 Liangmaqiao Road,
Chaoyang District（朝阳区亮马桥路
50 号凯宾斯基饭店 1 层）
Tel: 64653388 ext. 5732
Price: average RMB 200 per head
plus 15% service charge
Payment: cash or credit card
Hours: 11:00 am to 1:00 am

The brasserie imported its beer-making technology from the century-old Paulaner brewery in Munich. The diminutive glittering brewing equipment on the site goes well with the German designed wooden furniture, giving prominence to the august yet comfortable environment. Paulaner beer is made of imported malt using traditional German techniques. The whole brewing process takes four weeks, with no chemical ingredients used. The beer is light and refreshing, free from any bitter taste.

Every May and October the brasserie sets up festooned tents in the eastern garden, and hosts parties with performances by Bavarian bands. The merry scene will remind people of the streets of Munich.

Specialties

Kempinski Assortment 凯宾大拼盘
Roasted Pig's Knee 烤猪膝

【Roasted Pig's Knee 烤猪膝】

Le Pré Lenôtre, Sofitel Wanda

法餐厅

Restaurant Information

Address: 6th Floor, Sofitel Wanda Beijing, Tower C, Wanda Plaza, 93 Jianguo Road, Chaoyang District (朝阳区建国路 93 号万达广场 C 座北京万达索菲特大饭店 6 层)

Tel: 85996666 ask for "Le Pre Lenotre"

Price: average RMB 300 per head

Payment: cash or credit card

Hours: 11:00 am -10:00 pm

【Espresso Coffee 特浓咖啡】

Sofitel Wanda Beijing has introduced Le Pré Lenôtre, a Michelin three-star gastronomy house, with the aim of providing a cozy atmosphere for diners to enjoy French cuisine. In this restaurant, an extra space is set aside especially for smoking cigars. With experience working in certain famous French restaurants with Michelin ratings, the chefs specialize in French and Mediterranean cuisine. They have selected a range of specialty dishes for Le Pré Lenôtre by using superior ingredients and preparing them according to its rigorous standards. Perfection in everything, from choosing the ingredients, to the cooking process, through to serving on the table, is what Le PréLenôtre strives for.

The restaurant can offer lunch or dinner to as many as 40 people. It is equipped with exquisite, exclusive furniture, small yet comfortable dining tables along with elegant dinner sets, all adding an atmosphere of French graciousness, reflecting Le Pré Lenôtre's enduring elegant style, giving patrons a sense of joy as they listen to the French waiters introduce the gourmet items, as if finding themselves transported to the Champs Elysees in Paris.

"Michelin" is a French authoritative agency that appraises restaurants and awards culinary ratings. It enjoys the finest reputation, considered the "holy bible for world gourmet dining." Michelin uses a three-star system for recommending restaurants: one star, "worth a visit"; two stars, "worth a detour"; three stars, "exceptional cuisine, worth a special journey." Three stars are not too easily awarded to restaurants. Only those that are able to consistently attain high assessments during Michelin inspectors' secret visits can achieve three stars.

Specialties

Tomato in Jelly 鲜番茄汁软胶冻

Turbot with Almond and Capers
杏仁原汁多宝鱼

【Turbot with Almond and Capers
杏仁原汁多宝鱼】

Noble Court 悦庭

Restaurant Information

Address: Grand Hyatt Hotel Beijing, Oriental Plaza, 1 East Chang'an Avenue,

Dongcheng District（东城区东长安街1号东方广场东方君悦大酒店）

Tel: 85181234 ext. 6532 or 3822

Price: average RMB 200 per head, plus 15% service charge

Payment: cash or credit card

Hours: 11:30 am to 2:30 pm, 5:30-10:00 pm

　　　　brunch 10:30 am to 2:30 pm (weekends)

【Sliced Tuna, Grated Yam on Sushi Rice
金枪鱼配山药泥盖饭】

【Selection of Deluxe Sashimi 刺身套餐】

Specialties

Tempura Udon 天妇罗乌东面

Cha Soba 绿茶冷面

Selection of Deluxe Sashimi 刺身套餐

Assortment of Sliced Sashimi on
  Sushi Rice 玄界滩寿司盖饭

Sliced Tuna, Grated Yam on Sushi
  Rice 金枪鱼配山药泥盖饭

Redmoon Dessert 东方亮甜品

Fotiaoqiang 佛跳墙
  (steamed abalone with shark's fin
  and fish maw in broth)

Char-siu Pastry 香麻叉烧酥

Imperial Shrimp Dumplings
  悦庭虾饺皇

【Assortment of Sliced Sashimi on Sushi Rice
玄界滩寿司盖饭】

【Redmoon Dessert 东方亮甜品】

The Grand Hyatt Hotel sits in the Wangfujing commercial district in the heart of Beijing. Its Chinese-style restaurant, Noble Court, emulates the layout of an old-time patrician mansion. Its five banquet rooms can accommodate both company feasts and family gatherings.

The food features classic Cantonese dishes prepared by leading chefs from Hong Kong. Its signature Stewed Fish with Ginseng is an epitome of a Chinese chef's mastery in combining high nourishment with great taste. Even household Stuffed Tofu takes on a royal appearance after being fried and stewed with sliced white bamboo shoots, shredded red radish, green peas and cream-colored bamboo fungus. And no effort is spared on the desserts. My favorite is chopped mango and grapefruit drenched in sago and coconut sauce, which looks and tastes great.

Ritz-Carlton Gi Restaurant 金阁

Restaurant Information

Address: Ritz-Carlton Hotel, 18 Jinrong Street（金融街 18 号丽思卡尔顿酒店内）

Tel: 66016666 (ask for the restaurant)

Price: average RMB 300 per head, plus 15% service charge

Payment: cash or credit card

Hours: 11:00 am to 10:00 pm

As a 100-year-old luxury hotel, Ritz-Carlton has always emphasized its mission of "surpassing customers' expectations." Ritz-Carlton Gi has carried forward this principle in its decor and service as well as in its cuisine, as manifested in the surrounding relief marble walls interspersed with Chinese paintings done on silk, smiling waitresses wearing Chinese-style red-beaded bracelets, and the soy sauce and vinegar containers that each makes up half of an Eight Diagram pattern.

Gi's menu includes Beijing, Shandong, Sichuan, Shanghai, Guangdong, Zhejiang and Chaozhou cuisines. The Red Date and Dry Fish Maw Stew has a thick and smooth soup, with tasty tender ingredients that maintain their original flavor while complementing each other very well. The half-fat and half-lean Dongpo Pork looks lustrous and tastes delicious, and the fat is actually not greasy. Sugar-coated Yam Sticks taste both crisp and tender. The palatable Aloe-Longan-Pawpaw Stew is nutritious for the skin.

Specialties

Shengjue Deep-water Fish Head

生嚼深海大鱼头

Aloe-Longan-Pawpaw Stew

芦荟桂圆炖万寿果

【Lemon Sorbet Fruit Desset 柠檬冰霜水果盘】

【Fresh Fruit with Red Wine 水果包配红酒汁】

Sakura Japanese Restaurant
樱日餐厅

Restaurant Information

Address: 26 Jianguomenwai Street, Chaoyang District（建国门外大街 26 号）

Tel: 65125555 ext. 1226

Price: RMB 120-200 per head, plus 15% service charge

Payment: cash or credit card

Hours: breakfast 7:00 to 9:00 am, lunch 11:30 am to 2:00 pm, dinner 5:30-10:00 pm

The restaurant sits in the stately New Otani Changfugong Hotel by Chang'an Avenue, the main east-west thoroughfare in central Beijing. All its main chefs are from the renowned New Otani Hotel in Japan, and rotate on two-year terms. Most waiters/waitresses have received training in Japan, and the service is warm and polite.

【Tepanyaki 铁板烧】

The menu changes with the seasons, offering different specialties in different seasons: eel for summer, pine mushrooms (matsutake) for autumn, hotpot for winter, and sushi for spring. The pine mushroom is dubbed "the king of mushrooms." The restaurant presents pine mushroom entrees and ensembles every September and October, made with top-grade pine mushrooms from northeastern China.

The decor is typically Japanese. The huge ceiling-to-floor windows offer sights of the back garden, which is inundated with cherry blossoms in springtime.

Specialties

Tepanyaki 铁板烧

Soban Noodles with Green Tea 茶色荞麦面

Shabu-shabu 日式火锅

Assorted Vinegars 什锦酸物

Fried Conger Eel 炸星鳗

"Top Quality" with Vegetables 特选牛肉鸡素烧和素菜

Kobe Beef Grilled on Hot Stones 石烤特选牛肉

"Top Quality Beef" Special Selection Course 特选牛会席

【Soban Noodles with Green Tea 茶色荞麦面】

Sampan Restaurant 凯莱船餐厅

Restaurant Information

Address: 1st floor, Gloria Plaza Hotel Beijing, 2 Jianguomen South Street, Dongcheng District（建国门南大街 2 号凯莱大酒店 1 层）

Tel: 65158855 ext. 3155

Price: average RMB 150 per head, plus 15% service charge

Payment: cash or credit card

Hours: 11:00 am to 10:30 pm

Specialties

Pigeon Stuffed Bird's Nest 迷你鸽吞燕

Chicken, Abalone and Shark's Fin Soup 浓汤鸡鲍翅

Deep-fried Baby Pigeon 生炸乳鸽

Cantonese pastries 广东点心

The restaurant serves typical Cantonese cuisine, which is known for its broad range of hotpot and soup varieties. The masterpieces include Steamed Pork with Preserved Greens, Seafood and Tofu Clay-pot and Fish-head Clay-pot. The restaurant has a host of regular customers who bring friends and families for dimsum every weekend. The pull is the over 30 Cantonese snacks, including Durian Pastry, Carp Pudding, Hometown Wheat Pancakes and Bitter-melon Balls Soup.

Steak Exchange "巨"扒房

【Fried Crab-cakes with Tomato and Lemon Grass Salsa 蟹肉饼配蕃茄柠檬色拉】

【Chocolate Devil Cake 巧克力蛋糕】

Restaurant Information

Address: InterContinental Hotel, 11 Jinrong Street, east of Yuetan North Flyover（西城区金融街 11 号洲际酒店）

Tel: 58525888

Price: average RMB 200 per head, plus 15% service charge

Payment: cash or credit card

Hours: 11:00 am to 2:00 pm; 5:30-10:30 pm

As its Chinese name suggests, the steakhouse features big-portion steaks that are larger than those served in any other steakhouse in the city. The restaurant uses refrigerated fresh Angus beef imported from Australia. Angus beef is acknowledged worldwide as the best-quality beef and has a high content of protein. The tender, juicy and tasty steak is pleasing to the most refined palate. Rich chocolate and cheesecakes and other desserts are also indulgent temptations.

Steak Exchange is devoted to excellence. Its unique decor also provides diners with an impressive dining experience.

Specialties

Fried Crab-cakes with Tomato and Lemon Grass Salsa
蟹肉饼配蕃茄柠檬色拉

Chocolate Devil Cake 巧克力蛋糕

Summer Palace 夏宫

【Steamed Cuttlefish Dumplings 翡翠叶子饺】

【Winter Invigorant Soup 冬季滋补汤】

Restaurant Information

Address: 2nd Floor, China World Hotel, 1 Jianguomenwei Street, Chaoyang District（朝阳区建国门外大街 1 号中国大饭店 2 层）

Tel: 65012266 ext. 34

Price: average RMB 100-300, plus 15 % service charge

Payment: cash or credit card

Hours: 11:30 am to 2:15 pm; 6:00- 9:45 pm, night refreshments available until midnight

Specialties

Steamed Cuttlefish Dumplings
翡翠叶子饺

Taihu Black Pepper Turtle
太湖黑椒甲鱼

Chaozhou Shrimp Roll 潮州虾卷

Winter Invigorant Soup 冬季滋补汤

The Summer Palace restaurant on the second floor of China World Hotel is a haunt for lovers of dimsum brunch. Its masterpiece items include Preserved Egg and Pork Porridge, Flaky Pastries with Durian and Chestnut Paste, Steamed Beef Tendon and Shaomai (steamed dumplings) with fresh shrimp and crab stuffing.

The decor is classic Chinese. The splendid carpet, pendant lights and tableware fit well with the upscale hotel in which the site is located. There are performances of traditional Chinese music in the communal dining space.

Traders Café　三江咖啡厅

Restaurant Information

Address: Traders Hotel, 1
Jianguomenwai Street, Chaoyang
District（朝阳区建国门外大街1号国
贸饭店）
Tel: 65052277
Price: average RMB 158 per head,
plus 15% service charge
Payment: cash or credit card
Hours: 6:00 am to 11:00 pm

Traders Hotel occupies an advantageous location in Beijing's central business and embassy area. Its Traders Café features an array of Asian snacks that are popular with diners. In the Japanese cuisine section, fresh salmon, sushi, Arctic shellfish and tuna, all with equally fresh lemon, are great temptations to one's appetite. The desserts are also excellent. Cooled salty and sweet cheesecakes taste just great, while the Bah Kut Tea is genuinely Singaporean.

The café decor is in a succinct Western style, making it pleasant and comfortable. The open kitchen exhibits the culinary art of the chefs.

Specialty

Hainan Chicken Rice with Laksa
海南鸡饭

The Peninsula Beijing 皇庭

Address: B2, Beijing Palace Hotel, 8
Jinyu Hutong, Wangfujing （王府井
街金鱼胡同 8 号王府饭店 B2 层）
Tel: 85162888 ext. 6707
Price: average RMB 200 per head
plus 15% service charge
Payment: cash or credit card
Hours: 11:30 am to 2:30pm; 6:00 pm
to 1:00 am

The interior of the restaurant
is a modern interpretation of the
design of the Beijing hutong
(local dialect for alleyway) and

【Milk with Ginger Sauce 姜汁炖奶】

courtyard. The walls are built with gray bricks from demolished old residential buildings; the floor is paved with pinewood; the beams come from a 200-year-old mansion in Suzhou; and the rosewood furniture is of Ming-dynasty design. Many items in the hall are genuine antiques, such as the screen, stone windows, front door, and the door rings of the restroom. This classical air cannot be better captured than that in the tea room, where the finest tea is served in an artistic and tranquil environment.

The food is Cantonese cuisine, prepared by reputed chefs. Besides the wonderful entrees, the snacks and deserts are also mouth-watering. To name a few, the Dumplings Stuffed with Minced Shrimp and Pork, Mango Pudding, Sweet Green-bean Paste, Coconut Tart and Ginger Pudding. Refined setting, kingly service and imperial food — what more could you expect for a perfect meal?

Specialties

Huang Ting Chicken 杏片西柠鸡

Huang Ting Shark's Fin 浓汤黄焖鲍翅

Huang Ting Shrimp Shaomai 虾饺烧卖

Milk with Ginger Sauce 姜汁炖奶

【Huang Ting Chicken 杏片西柠鸡】

【Huang Ting Shark's Fin 浓汤黄焖鲍翅】

【Huang Ting Shrimp Shaomai 虾饺烧卖】

China's Renowned Liquors

Maotai

One of the world's three most celebrated liquors (together with Scotch whisky and French cognac), Maotai has a history of over 800 years. It is often used at state banquets, on diplomatic occasions or as an official gift. The refreshing liquor gives a sense of great pleasure. The aroma left in the glass lingers several days, long after the Maotai has been consumed.

Wuliangye

Wuliangye, a liquor made from sorghum, glutinous rice, corn, rice and wheat, possesses an exceptional pure, mild and mellow bouquet. It won the gold medal for best alcoholic beverage at the 1995 Panama International Trade Fair, and is regarded as one of the finest liquors available today.

Luzhou Laojiao

Luzhou Laojiao is one of the top liquors with strong aroma. Its cellar, named as a national treasure, has been listed in Guinness Record books as the world's oldest liquor cellar. Lu Zhou Laojiao is renowned mainly for two brands: Luzhou Laojiao 1573 and 100-year Luzhou Laojiao.

Fenjiu

Fenjiu is said to be produced in Xinghuacun, Fenyang County, Shanxi Province. It is representative of mildly aromatic liquors, characterized by its pure, sweet, and mild bouquet. Drinking it properly can drive away the cold, remove digestive retention and promote blood circulation.

Shuijingfang

Shuijingfang, China's first liquor workshop, is regarded as the oldest, most comprehensive and well-preserved distillery with original folk characteristics, nationwide and worldwide.

Gujing Gongjiu

The Gujing Gongjiu brand of liquor is produced in Gujing Distillery in Boxian County, Anhui Province. According to historical records, the liquor in its production used water from a well surviving from the Southern and Northern Dynasties (420-589). During the Wanli reign (1573-1620) of the Ming Dynasty, the liquor was sent to the emperor as tribute, thus earning its present name (Gujing, a place name; gong, "tribute", and jiu, liquor).

Yanghe Daqu

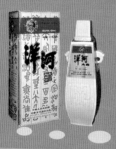

Yanghe Daqu, one of China's eight renowned liquors, has a history of over 300 years. It is characterized as sweet, soft, pure and aromatic.

Erguotou

Erguotou, a type of mildly aromatic liquor, originated from the strong brew of northern China. In order to improve the liquor quality, distilleries in Beijing developed its production technology, and discovered the liquor at its second distillation to be the sweetest and most aromatic. The liquor was thus named Erguotou (literally "head of the second pot"), to refer to the "second distillation." Beijing boasts Hongxing (Red Star) Erguotou and Niulanshan. There is a famous saying, "Three delights in Beijing are climbing the Great Wall, eating Quanjude roast duck, and drinking Hongxing Erguotou. It is hard to say you have been to Beijing without trying all three."

Business Dining

I speak from my experience of treating a good number of friends who come to Beijing from all around the globe on business or sightseeing trips. I believe that the question of what, where and how to feed them has much significance in the demonstration of my hospitality.

South Beauty Lan Club 俏江南

Restaurant Information

Address: 4th Floor, Shuangzi
Building, B12 Jianguomenwai Street,
Chaoyang District（建国门外大街乙
12 号双子大厦 4 层）
Tel: 51096012
Price: average RMB 500 per head
Payment: cash or credit card
Hours: 11:30 am to 2:00 pm; 5:30 to
2:00 am

【Stone Grilled Shrimps with Huadiao Wine in
Wooden Cask 木桶花雕茶烹凤尾虾】

Designed by renowned French architect Philippe Starck, South Beauty Lan Club is an embodiment of visual impact and the imagination of fine architecture. Here gastronomy teams up with fashion, delectability, luxury and the arts.

Every chandelier, oil painting or piece of furniture in the restaurant demonstrates a style of fashion and luxury. Of the Lan Club's more than 100 chandeliers, each is distinct from the other. A great number of famous Baroque painting reproductions look stunning hanging from the ceiling. Four long counters divide the restaurant into its Chinese, French, Indian and Mexican sections. While eating, diners can admire a variety of exhibits around them and indulge in a luxurious and artistic evening.

Specialties

Lan's Four Seasons (cold platter)
春夏秋冬十六拼

Royal Premium Shark's Fin and Abalone Soup 宫廷帝王翅

King Crab 皇帝蟹
(baked in rich stock and stir-fried with pepper-sand salt and steamed with egg white)

Sauteed Australian Abalone with Green and Red Peppers and Spicy Sauce Tasty Braised Crabs 回锅鲜鲍鱼

Stone Grilled Shrimps with Huadiao Wine in Wooden Cask 木桶花雕茶烹凤尾虾

【Sauteed Australian Abalone with Green and Red Peppers and Spicy Sauce Tasty Braised Crabs 回锅鲜鲍鱼】

【Lan's Four Seasons (cold platter) 春夏秋冬十六拼】

Shen Ji Soups 沈记靓汤

Restaurant Information

Address: 1 Xindong Road, Chaoyang

District（朝阳区新东路 1 号）

Tel: 65321177, 65321041

Price: average RMB 88 per head

Payment: cash or credit card

Hours: 11:00 am to 2:00 pm; 5:00

pm to 4:00 am

【Shark-fin and Meat Soup 沉鱼落雁】

Soup-cooking takes time and particular skill. Simmering for over 10 hours on a low fire is not uncommon, but by then, all the nutritious elements of the ingredients will have disappeared through the stock, rendering the ingredients themselves disposable. Because of the fastidiousness it takes to make soups, many restaurants would think twice about using the word in their name. Shen Ji Soups is an exception, turning soups into a culinary art, which has become its core.

Shen Ji Soups' Beijing branch specializes in Guangdong and Sichuan cuisines, and is devoted to developing and promoting healthy gourmet series based on nutritious ingredients, such as fungus, mushrooms, vegetables and fruits that are favored by health-and-diet-savvy urbanites.

Its Pig's Trotter and Aweto Soup is prepared from a secret recipe that uses various seasonings to make the two ingredients mutually complimentary and the soup both delicious and nutritious. The same with the Wax Gourd and Duck Soup, which is simmered over a low fire for many hours. A good soup is not judged by its price, but by its taste.

Specialties

Shark-fin and Meat Soup 沉鱼落雁

Fotiaoqiang 佛跳墙
  (steamed abalone with shark's fin
  and fish maw in broth)

Abalone and Chicken Stewed with
  Bamboo Shoot 竹笙鲍鱼炖老鸡

Shen Ji-style Panned Dumplings
  沈记特色生煎包

Lotus Root with Sweet Osmanthus
  Syrup 桂花糖藕

【Japanese Style Sea Cucumber 日式冰镇辽参】

【Assorted Meat Soup with Winter Melon
迷你八宝冬瓜盅】

Ah Yat Abalone 阿一鲍鱼

Restaurant Information

Address: 1st Floor, Jinzhiqiao Building, A1 Jianguomenwai Street, Chaoyang District （建国门外甲 1 号金之桥大厦 1 层）

Tel: 65089613

Price: average RMB 500 per head, plus 10% service charge

Hours: 10:30 am to 10:30 pm

This restaurant was opened by Hong Kong's most celebrated chef, Yeung Koon Yat, winner of the "CCC Gold Medal," presented by the Club des Chefs des Chefs (established by presidents' and kings' chefs around the world), and "Star of Excellence," by La Chaine des Rotisseurs. Such a supreme reputation in culinary culture deserves a taste. The restaurant's abalone dishes are truly a special treat, both to the palate and the eyes.

【Braised Sea Whelks with Dressing 葡汁响螺】

【Whole Ah Yat Oma Abalone 阿一原只日本窝麻鲍】

【Braised Supreme Shark 红烧海虎翅】

【Mexican Abalone 冰镇墨西哥鲍鱼】

【Alaska Crab with Goose Liver 黑椒鹅肝阿拉斯加蟹】

Specialties

Whole Ah Yat Oma Abalone

　阿一原只日本窝麻鲍

Alaska Crab with Goose Liver

　黑椒鹅肝阿拉斯加蟹

Braised Supreme Shark 红烧海虎翅

Braised Sea Whelks with Dressing

　葡汁响螺

Mexican Abalone 冰镇墨西哥鲍鱼

Tang Palace Seafood Restaurant
唐宫海鲜舫

Restaurant Information

Address: 3rd Floor, Xinqiao Hotel, 2 Dongjiaominxiang Street（东交民巷 2号新侨饭店3层）

Tel: 65129603, 65128926

Price: average RMB 150 per head

Payment: cash or credit card

Hours: 7:30 am to 10:30 pm

【Herbal Jelly (Guilinggao Powder) 龟苓膏】

Tang Palace Seafood Restaurant specializes in Hong Kong style dimsum and Guangdong seafood dishes. Once inside the restaurant, one feels as if having entered a marina, being surrounded by carefully positioned aquariums. A delicious meal midst a sea view makes for an impressive experience.

The seafood dishes at the restaurant are very good, as they are fresh, carefully prepared, and genuinely Cantonese in taste. There is also a wide choice of sweet desserts as well as salty savories. If fed up with butter and

【Steamed Rice Rolls with Shrimps 鲜虾肠粉】

cream, why not try these genuine Chinese desserts and snacks?

Specialties

Silver Codfish Braised with Scallions
葱烧银鳕鱼

Cuttlefish Braised in Seven-Flavor
Sauce 七味酱汁烧乌贼

Shatin Pigeons in Tanggong Style
唐宫沙田乳鸽

Cuttlefish and Foie Gras Tempura
天妇鹅肝酱炸墨鱼

Durian Pastry 飘香榴莲酥

Apricot Crystal Custard 杏香水晶糕

Crispy Shrimp Balls with Nuts
果仁脆虾球

【Pan-fried Turnip Patties 萝卜糕】

【Chicken Feet 凤爪】

【Carb Roe Dumplings 蟹黄小笼包】

Dintaifung 鼎泰丰

Restaurant Information

Address: Yibei Building, 22 Hujiayuan (adjacent to the Yuyang Hotel), Chaoyang District（胡家园22号迤北楼）

Tel: 64624502

Price: average RMB 100 per head

Payment: cash or credit card

Hours: Weekdays 11:30 am to 2:30 pm; 5:30pm to 10:00 pm, Weekends 11:00 am to 10:00 pm

Website: www.dintaifung.com.cn

Love *baozi* (steamed buns)? Then you shouldn't miss Dintaifung. The stuffing is made from the meat of pigs from trusted suppliers and slaughtered within the day. The skin is prepared with flour and chick broth, instead of water as elsewhere. The automatic *baozi* steamer, one of the only four in the world, ensures that each batch undergoes a heating process for precisely 4 minutes and 23 seconds.

The restaurant has sustained itself for 34 years on its *baozi* business. And it has preserved to date its humble setting, attentive service and passion to bring customers the best.

My favorite order is Crabmeat Steamed Dumpling, succulent meat encased in a porcelain-thin skin. It tastes even better after a dip in vinegar soaked with shredded ginger. According to the tastes of its northern patrons, Dingtaifeng has modified its recipe, making the buns less sweetish than those found at their origins in southern China. Another invention is to serve them in egg soup. Its chicken soup is peerless, easy on oil and tender in meat. And you will leave with regrets if you don't try out the dessert list.

Specialties

Steamed Eight Treasures Pudding 八宝饭

Steamed Vegetable and Pork Dumplings (10 pieces)菜肉蒸饺

Steamed Specialty Seafood Dumplings (10 pieces)海鲜小笼包

Steamed Shrimp and Pork Shaomai (10 pieces)虾肉烧麦

Double-boiled Chicken Soup 元盅鲜鸡汤

【Steamed Shrimp and Pork Shaomai 虾肉烧麦】

Lu Lu Restaurant 鹭鹭酒家

Restaurant Information

Address: A1 Ciyunsi, Chaoyang District, Beijing（朝阳区慈云寺甲 1 号）

Tel: 65080101, 65080505

Price: average RMB 100 per head

Payment: cash or credit card

Hours: 11:00 to 2:00 pm; 5:00-10:00 pm

【Steamed Dazha Crabs 大闸蟹】

【Stir-fried Shelled Shrimp 清炒虾仁】

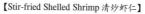

Lu Lu has 20 years of experience in providing Shanghai cuisine, and is one of the few authentic Shanghai-cuisine restaurants in the capital. To preserve the authenticity of its dishes, the restaurant employs chefs with a professional experience of at least 10 years, and all its main ingredients are flown in from Shanghai.

Lu Lu Restaurant's Dongfang branch is magnificently and uniquely decorated to reflect high-taste elegance and grace. The spacious hall is almost 10 meters tall. Sitting behind a plant or nestling in a seat by the window, diners can temporarily forget the clamor of the city as they savor gastronomic delights.

【Shanghai Sanhuang Chicken 上海三黄鸡】

【Sweet and Sour Ribs 糖醋小排】

【Sauteed Crab Fillet and Asparagus 蟹柳芦笋】

Specialties:

Stir-fried Shelled Shrimp 清炒虾仁

Shanghai Sanhuang Chicken
　上海三黄鸡

Sweet and Sour Ribs 糖醋小排

Sauteed Crab Fillet and Asparagus
　蟹柳芦笋

Merrylin 美林阁

Restaurant Information

Address: 8 Jianguomen North Street, Dongcheng District

（东城区建国门北大街 8 号）

Tel: 85191666, 85191777

Price: average RMB 100 per head

Payment: cash or credit card

Hours: 11:00 am to 2:30 pm; 5:00-9:30 pm

Merrylin specializes in Shanghai cuisine and is heralded as "Beijing's representative of Shanghai cuisine." Its dishes are masterfully prepared and most delicious. If you like pot-stewed food with a bit of sweet taste, Merrylin is the place. The chain restaurant follows its own culinary techniques that combine traditional ingredients with modern cooking skills, or modern ingredients with traditional cooking skills. Sweet and Sour Ribs is a classic Shanghai cold dish, but at Merrylin it is served hot, also tasting great after it gets cold. The Lotus Root Stuffed with Sweet Osmanthus-scented Glutinous Rice is just right in the sweetness and softness of the rice, with a lingering aftertaste of the aro-

【Green Mango KIWI 冰镇情人果】

【Braised Goose Feet and Mushrooms in Abalone Sauce 鲍鱼汁扣鹅掌杏鲍菇】

matic scent.

The restaurant decor features European elements. The portico, carpets, hanging TV sets and caressing lights enhance its luxury ambience. The tables are reasonably spaced, and the restaurant is not noisy.

Specialties

Green Mango KIWI 冰镇情人果

Braised Shark's Fin 红烧天狗翅

Iced Bitter Melon 冰镇苦瓜

【Iced Bitter Melon 冰镇苦瓜】

【Braised Shark's Fin 红烧天狗翅】

Wahaha Restaurant 娃哈哈

Restaurant Information

Address: 99 Longfusi Street,
Dongcheng District（东城区隆福寺
街 99 号）
Tel: 84095855/66/77
Price: average RMB 100 per head
Payment: cash or credit card
Hours: 10:00 am to 10:00 pm

Walking into the Wahaha Restaurant, one feels as if one were entering an elegant southern Chinese town of rivers: exquisite bridges over gurgling streams, lotus ponds, and southern-style lanes flanked by masterfully decorated dining compartments — an ambience enhanced by southern Chinese light music and palatable Hangzhou dishes.

The Hangzhou dishes are not greasy but taste delicious and a bit sweet. My favorite is Perch Wrapped in Tinfoil, a specialty of the restaurant. The flesh is very tender, and the sauce is pleasantly sweet and sour.

Wahaha's Casserole Dongpo Pork is also very good. It takes 18 steps to finish this dish, which uses cooking wine instead of water, and dark instead of light soy sauce. It is first braised for three hours, before being re-

【Pan-fried Beef Ribs 生煎牛仔排】

moved into a jar and baked, with dried Jiangxi bamboo shoots added, for another three hours. These preparations give the dish a brownish luster, and drain the fat of its grease.

Specialties

Pan-fried Shrimps 油爆虾

Hot and Sour Cuttlefish Roe Soup

酸辣乌鱼蛋汤

【Hot and Sour Cuttlefish Roe Soup 酸辣乌鱼蛋汤】

【Pan-fried Shrimps 油爆虾】

Zhang Sheng Ji 张生记

Restaurant Information

Address: 2nd and 3rd Floors, Zhejiang Hotel Annex Building, 12, Area 3, Anzhenxili, North Third Ring Road, Chaoyang District

（朝阳区北三环安贞西里3区12号浙江大厦裙房2、3层）

Tel: 64420006-8

Price: average RMB 80-100 per head

Payment: cash or credit card

Hours: 10:00 am to 11:00 pm

Hangzhou dishes are light and refreshing and pay attention to the use of seasonings, which are meant to compliment the main ingredient and not to dilute its flavor. Every traditional Hangzhou dish has a story behind it.

Longjing Shelled Shrimp is said to be related to Emperor Qianlong (reigned 1735-95). Once the emperor visited Hangzhou, disguised as an ordinary citizen, and had Longjing tea in a tea grower's home. The tea was aromatic and refreshing, so he took some tea leaves with him. When he dined at a restaurant in the city, he gave the leaves to a waiter, asking him to make him some tea with them. By accident, the waiter caught a glimpse of the dragon robe beneath Qianlong's plain robe and hurried to inform his boss — the restaurant owner. The proprietor was cooking a shrimp dish. He was so shocked by the news that he mistook the tea leaves in the waiter's hand as chopped scallion and dropped them into the wok. However, to his delight, the leaves gave the dish a nice color and unique taste. When Qianlong tried it, he was greatly pleased. Since then, Longjing Shelled Shrimp has become a famous Hangzhou dish.

Zhang Sheng Ji is an authentic Hangzhou restaurant. Its specialties, such as Duck and Dried Bamboo Shoots Casserole, Longjing Shelled Shrimp and Tofu with Crab Meat, are superb. The restaurant's folk-style decor creates a charming and comfortable ambience that enhances the diners' sensatory experience.

【Sweet Bean 特色甜豆】

Specialties

Slow Cooked Bamboo with Duck
笋干老鸭煲
Marinated Croaker 爆腌黄鱼
Sweet Bean 特色甜豆

【Slow Cooked Bamboo with Duck 笋干老鸭煲】

【Marinated Croaker 爆腌黄鱼】

Chinese Table Manners

Chopsticks are indispensable for a Chinese meal, and one should know the taboos around them.

No tapping: Don't tap a chopstick against the bowl, plate or cup, while eating or waiting for a meal to come.

No tossing: Before dinner, chopsticks are placed pair by pair in front of every diner, or passed around to each diner. If someone sitting on the other side of a table needs a pair, one should pass chopsticks over, rather than tossing them across the table.

No crossing: A pair of chopsticks should not be crossed, or placed with one thick side up and the other thick side down. They should be placed by the side of the bowl, instead of over it.

No sticking: When stopping eating for a while, one should place his/her chopsticks on the table, usually by the side of the plate, instead of sticking them into a dish or the rice.

No poking: When picking from a dish, one should not dig or poke it with chopsticks. If another person happens to select from the same dish, one should pull back his/her chopsticks to avoid a "chopstick collision."

No wielding: When speaking while eating, one should not wield his/her chopsticks as if using a knife. If a host wants to ask guests to help themselves, he/she should not gesture to do so by pointing his/her chopsticks at dishes.

"Seating order" comprises another major aspect of Chinese table manners at formal banquet. Generally speaking, the left or east side is superior to the right or the west side, demarcated by the most honorable seat that usually faces the door. At a family banquet, the most honorary seat is reserved for the eldest, while other members flank alternately left and right, according to their seniority. Toasting should also take turns as such. This rule applies to both long and round tables.

If it is a round table, the seat facing the door is reserved for the most honored person. To its left are respectively the second, fourth and sixth seats whereas to its right the third, fifth and seventh seats.

If it is a big square table that can seat eight people — two on each side — the first seat to the right of the table side that faces the door is reserved for the host. Down his/her left side are respectively the second, fourth, sixth and eighth seats; and right, the third, fifth and seventh seats.

At a multiple-table banquet, the central front table is the most honorary. To its left are the second, fourth or sixth tables if space allows, and to its right are the third, fifth or seventh in importance.

A Chinese dinner starts with cold dishes and beverages, followed by hot courses, staples, desserts and fruit. At a big banquet with many tables, all the tables should be served the same course in synch.

A dish is usually served in three manners: on a big plate, with diners taking turn to help themselves; a waiter/waitress helping diners to the dish by bringing it to each diner; or the dish being divided and placed in saucers, according to the number of diners.

Private Dining

A tranquil and congenial environment evokes a sweet nostalgia for the past. Take a seat in a fine restaurant, luxuriate while ordering leisurely, and even start some soul searching. There is no better way to hide away from the swirling din of urban life for a couple of hours.

Bellagio Café 鹿港小镇

【Hakka Saute 客家小炒】

Restaurant Information

Address: 6 Gongti West Road,
Chaoyang District （朝阳区工体西路
6 号）
Tel: 65513533
Price: average RMB 60 per head
Payment: cash or credit card
Hours: 10:30 am to 11:00 pm

【Pork Intestine Stewed with Ginger Slices
姜丝大肠】

Bellagio Café has an endearing Chinese name, "Little Lugang Town." Pop singer Luo Dayou's namesake song has spread the reputation of this 300-year-old small town in Taiwan across both sides of the Taiwan Straits. The restaurant is run by a Taiwanese entrepreneur. It is a relaxing and laidback place either for dinner, a cup of coffee, or a frozen dessert. Its red bean and mango frappes are highly recommended.

Bellagio Café incorporates the architectural style of European restaurants into its design, while its open layout, modernity and cheerfulness of decor inject even more liveliness to the small "town."

Specialties

Shrimp Wrapped in Deep-fried
Dough Twist Served with Pineapple
菠萝油条虾
Taiwan Tofu Casserole 台湾豆腐煲
Hakka Saute 客家小炒
Three-cup Chicken 三杯鸡

【Shrimp Wrapped in Deep-fried Dough Twist
Served with Pineapple 菠萝油条虾】

China Lounge 唐廊

【Deep-fried Codfish Taiwan Style 三杯银鳕鱼】

【Stir-fried Beef Fillet with Mushrooms 牛柳雪茸菇】

Restaurant Information

Address: southern gate of the
Workers' Gymnasium（工人体育场
南门内）
Tel: 65011166
Price: average RMB 100 per head
Payment: cash or credit card
Hours: 11:30 am to midnight

The restaurant is nestled under the foliage at the end of a gravel path by the southern gate of the Workers' Gymnasium. The crystal exterior is strikingly western, while the interior is palpably Chinese. French windows, massive square tables, a huge mosaic mural of flying goddesses and the spectacular chandelier make the space comfortably ritzy.

The food is adapted Cantonese cuisine featuring less oil and salt. The signature dish is Deep-fried Codfish Taiwan Style — crisp fish with thick sauce enclosed in three rings of onions. Pig Trotters with Mountain Treasures is also a must-try — succulent meat strewn with mushrooms and green vegetables.

The restaurant stores an extensive range of liquor of top Chinese and international names. In the lounge area customers can order a cup of tea or a glass of wine as they like, and admire the antiques around them.

Specialties

Duck Meat with Yolk Roll 蛋黄鸭卷
Deep-fried Codfish Taiwan Style
　三杯银鳕鱼
Poached Vegetables and Seafood in
　Clay Pot 玉液海皇煲
Stir-fried Beef Fillet with Mushrooms
　牛柳雪茸菇

Golden Jaguar Buffet 金钱豹

Restaurant Information

Address: 2nd Floor, Wangfu Century, 55 Dong'anmen Street, across from the Children's Theater (东安门大街 55 号王府世纪大厦 2 楼)

Tel: 65598888

Price: Lunch 11:00 am to 2:30 pm: RMB 180 per head; Dinner 5:00-8:00 pm: RMB 220 per head; 8:00-10:30 pm: RMB 180 per head

Payment: cash or credit card

Hours: 11:00 am to 10:30 pm

【Fashion Imagination Sushi Mix & Collection 创意寿司集锦】

【Japanese Seafood Champion Selection 日式海霸王】

If you want an international buffet, make your way to Golden Jaguar. Its nine sections of distinct culinary styles offer more than 400 dishes, including Alaska snow-crabmeat and French foie gras in the western section; ice-cooled large oysters and salmon in the Japanese section, tempura in the miscellaneous section; Casseroled Oyster and Abalone and Shark's Fin Soup in the Chinese section; Satays and Thai curries in the Southeast Asian section; and the crisp roasted piglet in the roast section; just to name a few. Your mouth will be watering just by looking on, or smelling these delicacies. The appetizing temptations do not end there. There

is an assortment of Western and Chinese desserts to follow, such as Tiramisu, chocolate brownies, tarts and durian. There is also a wide choice of drinks and ice-creams available in the beverage section. Be sure to take no more than you can eat, so you'll not waste these delicacies. I usually go on a diet the next day, after a visit to the Golden Jaguar, as my philosophy of reasonable diet has taught me.

Specialties

Alaska Snow Crabmeat
阿拉斯加雪蟹肉
French Foie Gras 法式鹅肝酱
Sashimi 生鱼片
Roasted Piglet 烤乳猪
Geoduck 象拔蚌

【Scallop in Shell in Abalone Sauce 鲍汁扣扇贝王】

【Taisu Food Club Steak 台塑牛小排】

Gourmet Room 古镇煌

【Steamed Conpoy in a Carrot Ring 银环瑶柱脯】

【Steamed Creamed Egg-white with Seafood 海鲜蒸乳酪】

Restaurant Information

Address: 3 Qianhai West Street, Shichahai, Xicheng District（西城区什刹海前海西街 3 号）

Tel: 66139641

Price: RMB 100 each for lunch; RMB 300, 350 or 500 each for dinner. Reservation is necessary if over RMB 500.

Payment: cash

Hours: Lunch, only Thursday to Sunday, Dinner 6:00-10:00 pm

This Hong Kong cuisine restaurant exceeds its peers in offering a full collection of the finest dishes from the region, beyond even what one could expect in Hong Kong. Its owner Koo Chun Wong, a Hong Kong writer, is a good friend of many local chefs, and therefore has been privileged to find the best recipes for the items on his menu.

The setting is of a modest but cultured style, reflected in its sign-board — a small white plaque with ancient-style calligraphy that reads "First-class Hong Kong Cuisine of Home Recipes." The huge windows in the dining space offer a full view of the courtyard with a fancy glass house used as a study. The study holds a good collection of books on various themes, such as travel, music, photography and curios, including books by the owner. Antique items, such as models of vintage cars and an ancient typewriter, can be seen scattered around the room, bringing visitors' minds back for decades.

Specialties

Steamed Creamed Egg-white with Seafood 海鲜蒸乳酪

Steamed Conpoy in a Carrot Ring 银环瑶柱脯

Hado Tepanyaki Cuisine
花渡铁板烧

【Kobe Beef Steak 神户牛排】

Restaurant Information

Address: 3rd Floor, Kuntai International Building, Chaowaidajie Street
（朝外大街昆泰国际大厦 3 层）
Tel: 58797188, 58797166
Price: RMB 188 per head for unlimited buffet; set meals and orders also available
Payment: cash or credit card
Hours: 11:00 am to 2:00 pm; 5:00-10:00 pm
Website: www.hado.com.cn

Specialties

Enoki Mushroom and Beef Roll
　金针菇牛肉卷
Kobe Beef Steak 神户牛排
Fried Pork Steak 炸猪排

【Fried Pork Steak 炸猪排】

Hado specializes in Japanese cuisine and French-style Tepanyaki. The iron plate used to cook the Tepanyaki reaches a temperature of 300 °C, so the surface of beef can be done quickly while its nutritious elements and original taste are preserved to the maximum. Then the beef is cooked further with sauce and wine, and cut into small pieces for easy eating. Half-done steak is the best in taste. Though salt is an indispensable ingredient for grilling, the amount used is very small. A steak thus cooked is good for the health and authentic in taste.

The buffet at the center of the Hado hall serves more than 180 dishes, and the surrounding red wine stalls offer different international brands. There are large iron plates in every dining section where chefs make the Tepanyaki right in front of diners, according to their requests.

Le Quai 有璟阁

Restaurant Information

Location: across from the No. 12
auditorium of the Workers
Gymnasium, Chaoyang District（朝
阳区工人体育场内 12 号看台对面）
Tel: 65511636/65511639
(reservation necessary)
Price: average RMB 150-200 per head
Hours: Lunch 11: 00 am to 2:00 pm;
Afternoon tea 2:30-5:00 pm; Dinner
5:00-10:30 pm; Bar 10:30 pm to 2:00 am

【Marine Mushrooms with Mustard 海磨菇芥菜胆】

Le Quai's steel-structured exterior belies its classic Chinese interior. The house is a 220-year-old mansion originally belonging to an Anhui official, and was reconstructed into a perfect East-meets-West concoction. The spacious lobby, six meters in height, displays splendid Hui-style woodcarvings. The pillars and rails display glazed glamour after centuries of scrubbing, echoing the restaurant's Chinese name, "You Jing" ("you"means "having" while "jing" refers to fine jade). Bronze-colored curtains of metal fragments separate the Chinese spaces from the western.

Private Dining

【Australian Stone Grill Rib-eye Steak 澳洲火山石牛眼排】

【Boston Lobster with Wild Mushroom Sauce 野菌汁佐波士顿龙虾翅】

The restaurant sits by a lake, and offers a lovely view through the glass wall facing the water.

In May 2006, Le Quai became the first Chinese affiliate of "Slow Food Italy," an eco-gastronomic organization that opposes fast-food. The cooking is conducted completely manually, and the ingredients are free of anything canned or genetically modified. Eating slowly provides a respite from the daily rush of the big city. There is a gallery named "Now" on the second floor. A stroll around to gaze at the art-works has the effect of lifting one's spirits, and consequently stirring the appetite.

Specialties

Boston Lobster with Wild Mushroom Sauce 野菌汁佐波士顿龙虾翅

Veggie Fish Fillet 水煮素鱼片

Salted Chicken Baked over Bamboo Charcoals 竹炭盐嫩鸡

Australian Stone Grill Rib-eye Steak 澳洲火山石牛眼排

Marine Mushrooms with Mustard 海蘑菇芥菜胆

【Veggie Fish Fillet 水煮素鱼片】

My Humble House 寒室

Restaurant Information

Address: 2nd Floor, Clubhouse 19, China Central Place, 89 Jianguolu, Chaoyang
District （朝阳区建国路 89 号华贸中心会所 19 号楼 2 层）

Tel: 65307770   Price: average RMB 200 per head

Payment: cash or credit card   Hours: 11:00 am to 2:30 pm; 5:00-10:30 pm

A modern-style Chinese restaurant, House by the Park is a fine-dining experience of delicate Chinese dishes served with Western etiquette, amidst a chic and comfortable ambience.

My favorite is the cold abalone and shark's fin named after the restaurant. The ingredients are pre-prepared by a special procedure and then put into the freezer, before they are marinated in XO sauce and Japanese vinegar and soy sauce. The coolness and tenderness of the dish generates a pleasant feeling. Rack of Lamb, which goes with turnip rice-cakes, is also very good. New Zealand lamb is first marinated and then sauteed on both sides. Bordeaux wine is added to enhance the taste.

Designed by MYU from Tokyo, House by the Park manifests a natural, simple and unique beauty that generates feelings of warmth, amicableness yet exclusivity. Its lighting uses famous German lamp designer Ingo Maurer's designs to create an electric wonderland. Diners can feast their eyes on Ingo Maurer's "Zettel" and "Birdie,"

and Italian Belux's "Jingzi." Belux has creatively developed a lighting system that plays a decisive role in building up the environment one desires. Top-class tableware produced by Germany's Robbe & Berking adds further refined touches to the restaurant.

Specialties

Grilled Lamb Chop with Red Wine Sauce 红酒烤羊排

Crabmeat and Spinach 蟹肉菠菜

Seafood Soup Wien Coconut Milk 椰奶海鲜汤

183

【Seafood Soup with Coconut Milk 椰奶海鲜汤】

Passby Restaurant 与食巨近

Restaurant Information

Address: 114 South Luoguxiang Hutong, Jiaodaokou, Dongcheng District（东城
交道口南锣鼓巷 114 号）

Tel: 64006868

Price: RMB 50-120 per head

Hours: 11:00 am to midnight

Website: www.passbybar.com

The restaurant is located in a big courtyard house hidden behind a small gate, deep in the labyrinth of the 700-year-old South Luoguxiang Hutong. At the entrance there is a prominent photo, taken by an Australian photographer, of a young lady in Peking Opera, printed on a 3m-long silk streamer that hangs from the top of the building. On the second floor, the dining compartments flanking the stairway symmetrically are decorated in romantic Chinese red, and even the air-conditioner is painted red. The restaurant has a compact coziness. If you open your window that faces the stairway, you may start an intimate chat with diners in the compartments across the way.

The restaurant serves "dishes that are closest to gastronomic art." My favorite is foie gras and Sesame Leaves served with champagne jelly, whose light taste goes very well with the bittersweet liver pate. The restaurant's masterly culinary procedure preserves the fresh taste of ice-cold codfish, which tastes just delicious when mixed with its secret creamy sauce. The mango and cream brownie wrapped in thin, crisp syrup and served with strawberry ice-cream is also superb.

Specialties

Foie Gras 鹅肝

Meat Grilled on Volcanic Stones 火山石扒肉

Mutton-cubes Pizza 羊肉串比萨

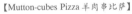

【Meat Grilled on Volcanic Stones 火山石扒肉】

【Mutton-cubes Pizza 羊肉串比萨】

186

Renjian Xuanba 人间玄八

Address: Millennium, 18 Jianguomenwai Street, Chaoyang District (朝阳区建国门外大街 18 号嘉华世纪)

Tel: 65158585

Price: average RMB 250 per head   Payment: cash or credit card

Hours: lunch, 11:30 am - 2:30 pm; dinner, 5:30 pm - 11:00 pm; cocktails, 11:30 am - 2:00 pm

"Renjian Xuanba," a name implying mystique, is a Beijing branch of Shintori, a renowned Japanese restaurant in Taipei. It offers a fusion of creative Chinese cuisine as well as Japanese cuisine. Dishes with light tastes and elegant vessels delight the diners. A stone path leads to the restaurant where customers, after zigzagging through a dark corridor, will find a bar and then a bright hall, with sunlit bamboo transplanted from China's south. With the bamboos swaying around them, diners soak up a sense of romance as if in the midst of gorgeous scenery south of the Yangtze River.

Specialties

Sizzling Stir-fried Beef on an Iron Plate 铁锄牛肉
Roast Fish with Miso and Buckwheat 人间豆腐
Spareribs with Plums 荞麦味噌烤鱼
Foie Gras 梅子排骨

Rose House 玫瑰园

Restaurant Information

Address: 1st Floor, Commercial
Building, Global Trade Mansion, A9
Guanghua Road, Chaoyang District
（朝阳区光华路甲9号世贸国际公寓
商务楼一层）
Tel: 65928688
Price: average RMB 50-100 per head
Payment: cash
Hours: 11:30 am to 10:00 pm

Founded in 1990, the Rose
House lives by the authenticity
of British afternoon tea. Enjoying
the set-menu Victorian afternoon
tea at Rose House, you can experience for yourself the refined
elegance of British gourmet
culture: coffee made by a Nea-
politan coffeemaker, beverages
made from fruit juice imported
from France, milk tea brewed by
using imported Whittard tea
leaves, and various kinds of purely
British cookies. Rosewater is

made from imported rose juice extracted from more than 10 kinds of rose, and every cup of rosewater contains the juice of 15 rose flowers. By adding a few cubes of ice, the drink becomes even more refreshing. My personal favorite is the flavored milk tea.

British tea, porcelain and art constitute the three themes of Rose House. What an experience to sip tea from a royal Aynsley cup as one watches the display of rose-themed paintings, listening to soothing music, or chatting with friends in air in which wafts the sweet scent of roses.

Specialties

Rose Tea 玫瑰茶

Biscuits 饼干

Earl Gray Tea 伯爵茶

Fruit Tea 水果茶

Santosa Tea Garden 圣陶沙茶楼

Restaurant Information

Address: A1 Waiguan Xiejie Street,
Andingmenwai, Chaoyang District
（朝阳区安定门外外馆斜街甲 1 号）
Tel: 85285000, 85285020
Price: average RMB 200 per head
Hours: 10:00 am - 1:00 am the
next morning

Unlike its name might suggest, dinner is actually the mainstay at Santosa, while tea is its sideline. The old photos, oil lamps and gramophones, with stacks of old records, distinguish the nostalgic and romantic design of the restaurant. A karaoke hall on the third floor is reserved for lovers of old songs, where there are renditions every evening. Listening to old songs over tea or dinner reminds one of a 1930s or 1940s Shanghai restaurant.

Santosa specializes in Guangdong cuisine, and also serves French and Russian dishes. Of its teas, Pu'er is the best.

Specialties

Tuna Sashimi 金枪鱼刺身

French Escargots 法式蜗牛

Lovers' Rose Tea 情人玫瑰茶

Sculpting in Time Café 雕刻时光

Restaurant Information

Address: 1st floor, No. 12 Building,
Huaqingjiayuan, Wudaokou,
Chengfu Road（成府路五道口华清嘉
园12号楼1层）
Tel: 82867025/82867026
Price: average RMB 30 per head
Payment: cash
Hours: 9:30- 0:30 am

The name, full of spiritual meaning, is borrowed from the biography of Andrei Tarkovsky, celebrated film director of the former Soviet Union. It was originally meant that cinematography records the flow of time, leaving sculpted marks on everything and everyone in the world. The café is imbued with nostalgia, yet in no way gloomy.

Mostly located near universities and colleges, the franchise cafés have among its patrons a large proportion of students, who add an infectious lively ambience.

The air is permeated with the aroma of coffee and herbal teas. Wooden floors and furniture, old books and photographs, rustic handicrafts... My mind always slips back to the good old days in a place like that.

Specialties

Cheesecake 芝士蛋糕

Pizza 比萨

Coffee 咖啡

Shan Zhai 善斋

Restaurant Information

Address: 2nd Floor, North Wing of Rainbow Plaza, 16 East Third Ring North Road, 200m north of Changhong Bridge, on the east side of the Third Ring Road

（东三环北路16号隆博广场北楼二层）

Tel: 65951199

Price: average RMB 200 per head

Payment: cash or credit card

Hours: 11:30 am to 10:00 pm

【Shan Zhai Golden Salad 善斋黄金沙拉】

Shan Zhai is an organic food restaurant, recommended by the organizing committee of the Organic China Expo. Shan Zhai lives by its maxim that, "Under no circumstance shall any food and drink that is harmful to people's health be presented to

our guests, no matter how delicious it is." Shan Zhai specializes in Japanese cuisine and vegetarian dishes. Its sushi is mostly made of coarse grains whose taste is refined by palatable ingredients, so neither taste nor nutrition is compromised. Organic vegetable salads and stir-fried greens — all using low-fat olive oil — along with vegetarian desserts and nutritious soups, cooked according to medicinal dietary theory, all generate a pastoral romantic air.

Shan Zhai's decor reflects traditional Chinese aesthetics. Going through its entrance, one will see an antique-style wooden gateway tower. The four characters carved on it read "Boruo Heart Sutra," with Buddhist implications. The second floor has an eye-goggling spaciousness — about 1,000 square meters in size and a height of 9 meters. The original-colored cement floor and tables and chairs compose a natural simplicity. A 2m-tall glittering ice Buddha statue sits in the center of the hall beneath an ancient bronze bell. The ice statue is replaced at 5:00 pm every day. The gradually thawing ice Buddha reflects the changeability of life. It is the way of Nature that people should follow as a philosophy of life.

【Glossy Ganoderma and Morchella Esculenta Casserole 竹笙灵芝褒羊肚菌】

【Five-millet Sushi 五谷寿司】

Specialties

Five-millet Sushi 五谷寿司

Shan Zhai Golden Salad 善斋黄金沙拉

Glossy Ganoderma and Morchella

Esculenta Casserole 竹笙灵芝褒羊肚菌

The American Café 博平咖啡

Address: 1st Floor, Lanbao International Condo Clubhouse, 3 West Dawang Road, Chaoyang District
（朝阳区西大望路 3 号蓝堡国际公寓会所一层）
Tel: 85997428/9
Price: RMB 50-100 per head
Hours: 9:00 am to midnight

【Green Chef Salad with Italian Dressing
厨师长沙拉】

The American Café is purely American — hamburgers, sandwiches, salads, pizza, spaghetti and steak for a decent brunch or dinner, accompanied by freshly made coffee and fruit juice.

The decor of the restaurant is nostalgic yet modern, passionate yet calm, as reflected in its scarlet fascia, glazed wooden tables and chairs, decorative colors of yellow, orange and red, and portraits of US presidents and impressionistic paintings that strew its walls — all against the background music of jazz or blues.

【Fruit Yougurt 什锦水果酸奶】

Specialties

Croissant 牛角包早餐拼盘

Honey Chicken Hamburgez

蜂蜜鸡肉汉堡

Fruit Yougurt 什锦水果酸奶

Cowboy Hamburger 牛仔汉堡

【Honey Chicken Hamburger 蜂蜜鸡肉汉堡】

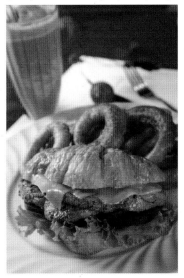

【Croissant 牛角包早餐拼盘】

Wang Steak House 王品台塑牛排

Restaurant Information

Address: 1st Floor, Miyang Building, Yong'andongli, East Chang'an Avenue, across from the south doors of Guiyou Store（东长安街永安东里米阳大厦首层）

Tel: 65680180, 65669228 (with designated parking lot)

Price: RMB 198 per head for seven courses (bread, salad, soup, main fare, supplementary fare, dessert and beverage), plus 10% service charge

Payment: cash or credit card

Hours: 11:30 am to 2:00 pm; 5:30-9:00 pm

This is a Western-style restaurant whose decor reflects European classical elegance and luxurious romance, as shown in the spaciousness of the restaurant, its comfortable and luxurious chairs, and romantically designed metal window-traceries, stained glass, fountain, and chandeliers.

Meticulous about its culinary art, Wang Steak House finally came to fruition after thousands of hours spent on research and development of its own recipe: only the three pairs of the sixth, seventh and eighth ribs of the cattle can maintain 100 percent of their juiciness and tenderness after being marinated for two days and nights with 72 Chinese and Western seasonings and baked for an hour and half in an oven at 250°C. And their portions are just right, at 17 cm long and weighing 16 ounces. So a head of cattle can produce only six portions of Wang Steak.

Shrimp and Asparagus Iced Salad contains scarlet shrimps served on transparent ice in a cocktail cup, set off by jade-green asparagus and lettuce and bright yellow yogurt-curry sauce — most delightful looking. The bread, fresh from the oven, is also very delicious, with a dip of the hot mushroom cheese sauce made by the restaurant itself. Try a hot chocolate Lava after the main fare. You can feel the warmth of the smooth hot chocolate going through your body, as well as the gentle sting of the ice-cream.

Specialties

Palmleaf Raspberry Fruit Sherbet

覆盆子沙瓦

Crystal Syrup Fruit Ice Cream

焦糖水果冰淇淋

Wang Steak 王品台塑牛排

【Palmleaf Raspberry Fruit Sherbet 覆盆子沙瓦】

Xiaowang's Home 小王府

Restaurant Information

Address: 6 Ritan North Road, Chaoyangmenwai, Chaoyang District, east of the North Heavenly Gate, inside Ritan Park（朝阳区朝阳门外日坛北路 6 号）
Tel: 85615985, 85617859
Price: average RMB 150 per head
Payment: cash or credit card
Hours: 10:00 am to 2:00 pm; 4:00-10:00 pm
Website: www.xiaowanghome.com

The proprietor's name is Wang Xiaowang, who so named his restaurant to aim at a home atmosphere for its patrons. Xiaowang's Home is known for "homemade dishes," which seem to be regular dishes, but are actually distinctive of this special restaurant. The most distinguished item at Xiaowang's Home might be the Choice Apricot-wood Roast Duck. It uses force-fed Beijing ducks, which have a thick layer of fat beneath the skin, and whose meat is juicy and tender. Apricot trees are hard and solid in texture due to the slowness of their growth, and an apricot fire generates a higher heat than regular woods, without burning the ducks, so they can be roasted for a longer time to absorb the aroma of the wood. A special pre-preparation requires the use of wild bees' honey on the ducks' skin. The sauce that goes with the roast duck is made from Liubiju soybean paste, which is further processed by being stewed with more than 20 extra ingredients. Instead of the traditional roasting duration of 45 minutes, the

【Boiled Duck Liver with Salt 咸水鸭肝】

ducks at Xiaowang's Home are roasted for a longer period, so they are less greasy and more tender.

Xiaowang's Home's Ritan Teahouse is inside the Ritan Park. The tall woods that surround it make it even more like being at home in a shaded traditional courtyard.

Specialties

Roast Duck 极品果木烤鸭

Dry Fried Craker 干烧黄鱼

Boiled Duck Liver with Salt 咸水鸭肝

【Roast Duck 极品果木烤鸭】

【Dry Fried Craker 干烧黄鱼】

【Sauteed Diced Chicken with Macadamia Nuts 王府夏果炒黄鸡】

Yuanding Tepanyaki 原鼎

Restaurant Information

Address: B1 Dongliang Building, 8 Deshengmen East Street, Xicheng District

（西城区德胜门东大街8号东联大厦）

Tel: 84080058, 84080028

Price: average RMB 500 per head; set meals ranging from RMB 400-1,600

available at dinner, and business luncheons around RMB 200 also available

Payment: cash or credit card

Hours: 10 am to 2:00 pm; 5:30-10:00 pm

【Beef Roll of French-style Foie Gras 鹅肝牛肉卷】　【Sauteed Foie Gras 鲜煎鹅肝】

Yuanding offers dining in private rooms only. No matter whether they are large or small, all the compartments are carefully decorated to embody Yuanding's care for its patrons.

Yuanding's French-style Tepanyaki follows the French royal procedure, and is composed of soup, seafood, vegetable, meat and dessert. The French-style Foie Gras and Beef Roll is a must-try. Foie Gras is first grilled on an iron plate, and then beef is added. The two different aromas mingle very well. Sizzling Cheese Lobster brings both a visual and gastronomical onslaught. The iron plate preserves the original delicate flavor of the lobster, enhanced by specially prepared honey mustard.

Specialties

Beef Roll of French-style Foie Gras
鹅肝牛肉卷

8A-Class Steak 8A 级牛排

Sizzling Cheese Lobster 铁板芝士龙虾

Sizzling Steak 铁板肋眼牛排

Sauteed Foie Gras 鲜煎鹅肝

【Sizzling Cheese Lobster
铁板芝士龙虾】

【Sizzling Steak 铁板肋眼牛排】

【8A-Class Steak 8A 级牛排】

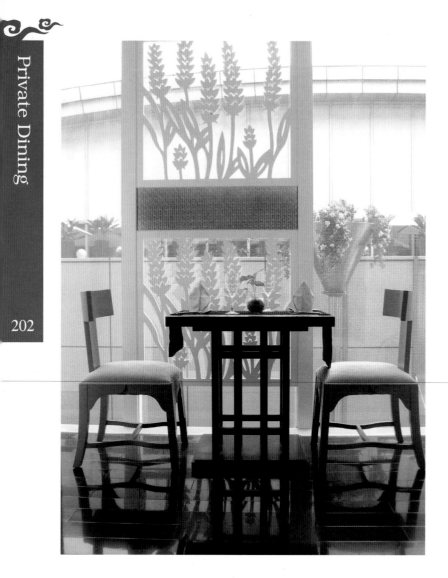

Zone de Confort 逸生活

Restaurant Information

Address: 4 Gongti North Road, Chaoyang District（朝阳区工体北路4号院内）

Tel: 65008070

Price: average RMB 100 per head

Payment: cash or credit card

Hours: 11:00 am to 10:30 pm

When I first heard of the restaurant, I was fascinated by its name. "De Confort" reminds me of a laid-back ambience and a leisurely tempo of life. I decided to go there to verify the tantalizing vision of my mind's eye.

My immediate impression of the restaurant was its powerful exoticism — Thai wooden sculptures, Venice-style framed pictures, Indian cushions, windows dressed with French lavender designs, teak pillars commonly seen on Bali Island, and especially the dark-brown teak tables with their Japanese-style mosaic ceramic tops, with matching 18th century-style aristocratic peach-wood chairs.

The restaurant has an open kitchen, so diners can watch how chefs prepare their meals. Bali Island Tuna Salad is very tasty, after being marinated for an entire night in local seasonings.

Fresh Mushrooms Fried with Vegetables and Black-fungus-stuffed Steamed Chicken, served with spicy kidney beans, are also very delicious. Their stuffed poultry recipe has more than a 100-year history and is particularly popular in central France. The complicated preparation preserves the juiciness and tenderness of the meat and gives it a wonderful taste that is matched and enhanced by the spicy beans, the crisp fungus and the delectable diced foie gras.

Specialties

Tuna Salad 金枪鱼沙拉

Seafood Garden Salad 海鲜田园沙拉

Tiramisu 提拉米苏

Banana Beef 香蕉牛肉排

Black-bean Fish 黑豆鱼

【Black-bean Fish 黑豆鱼】

【Banana Beef 香蕉牛肉排】

Seasonal Dietary Regimen

Seasonal dietary regimen emphasizes appropriate intake of food and tonics in accordance to the changes of the season, in order to strengthen one's body and health.

Spring Regimen

In spring, people should take foods that are mild and sweet in nature and rich in proteins, saccharides, vitamins and minerals, such as lean meat, egg, milk, honey, bean products, fresh vegetables and fruits. These foods will improve body tone and increase strength. People of weak health can take some mild tonics, such as American ginseng, dried longan, *dangshen* (Codonopsis pilosola) and root of membranous milk vetch.

Summer Regimen

In summer, the human body is physiologically energetic, while the weather is hot, so people should have a light diet and stay away from foods that tend to build up the inner heat of the body, such as greasy and fried foods. Vegetables that have a bitter taste can usually help reduce inner heat. Therefore, people should often eat these in summer to reduce heat and fatigue that accumulate in the body. Bitter beverages, such as beer, green tea and *kuding* (broadleaf holly leaf) tea, are also good for the body in summer.

Autumn Regimen

Traditional Chinese medicine advises nourishing of the *yang* in spring and summer, and of the *yin* in autumn and winter. Autumn is a good season to build up one's health, so people should pay attention to obtaining nutrition by taking mild foods.

Autumn is a dry season, so people should also have food that helps nourish the *yin*, moisten the lungs and enrich body fluids, such as pears, sesame, rock sugar, honey and tremella. Old people and those with weak stomachs should stay away from cold and tough foods.

Winter Regimen

To fend off the frigidity of winter, people should take warm-natured foods that help disperse cold and boost the *yang*. But these foods are high in heat that may accumulate in the lungs, causing excessive lung heat, as manifested by a dry mouth and tongue. Traditional Chinese medicine, therefore, advises using cold-natured food to counteract the heat. For example, turnip is mild in nature and has the function of smoothing the flow of vital energy, boosting digestion and reducing phlegm. If it is added to a beef stew, it can balance the "hotness" of the beef, and help strengthen vital energy and digestion.

Siheyuan Courtyard Gastronomy

Cupping a bowl of hot soup in my hands and watching the dancing snowflakes outside the windows, I was enamored with the sensual and visual beauty of the Chinese courtyard lifestyle. It was the second time that I spent the lunar New Year in Beijing, and this was one of the most wonderful experiences in my life.

Beiji Ge 北极阁

Address: 24 Beijige Santiao,
Dongdan North Street, Dongcheng
District（东城区东单北大街北极阁三
条二十四号院）
Tel: 65228288
Price: RMB 300 and up per head
Payment: cash
Hours: 11:00 to 2:00 pm;
　　　　5:00-10:00 pm

【Supreme Shark's Fin Served with Rice
北极阁招牌极品翅泡饭】

Walk along Silver Street at
Dongdan and turn east at the first
lane, and a few minutes later on
your right, you will find yourself
in front of a double red gate. The
only thing over the gate is a pair
of red lanterns.

It is a quiet oasis tucked away
from the bustle of downtown
Beijing. A huge, half-transparent
sunshade shelters the entire
courtyard, and the spring sun
sifts through it, embracing with
its caressing warmth.

The dark-tiled roofs and gray
walls tell the 100-year-old his-

tory of the restaurant. During the 1930s and 1940s, it was the residence of the chairman of the Chamber of Commerce of Chinese Russian Merchants and was often visited by local celebrities, including the four greatest *dan*-role actors of Peking Opera.

When night falls, the courtyard is illuminated by red lanterns, and echoes with background music, reminding one of bygone times.

The restaurant specializes in authentic Beijing aristocratic cuisine, featuring such delicacies as bird's nest, abalone and shark's fin. One of its best items is the Shark's Fin Served with Rice. The restaurant is also famous for its Guizhou cuisine and Pu'er tea. It makes for a nice afternoon spent sipping the tea in the courtyard.

【Ribs Sauteed with Fermented Bean Sauce and Served in a Miniature Pumpkin Dongpo Pork Casserole 秘制罐焖东坡肉】

Specialties:

Abalone and Sea Cucumber with Abalone Sauce 鲍汁扣鲍鱼辽参

Supreme Shark's Fin Served with Rice 北极阁招牌极品翅泡饭

Crispy Prawn 脆皮大明虾

Braised Seafood and Tofu 海鲜口袋一品豆腐

Ribs Sauteed with Fermented Bean Sauce and Served in a Miniature Pumpkin Dongpo Pork Casserole 秘制罐焖东坡肉

Fangshan Restaurant 仿膳

Restaurant Information

Address: 1 Wenjin Street, Xicheng District, inside east entrance of Beihai Park（西城区文津街 1 号北海公园东门内）

Tel: 64011889, 65011879

Price: average RMB 150 per head

Payment: cash

Hours: 11:00 am to 7:30 pm

Located in the former imperial garden — now Beihai Park — the 80-year-old restaurant is famed for its imperial-style cuisine, its name suggesting that its cuisine duplicates imperial dinners. The restaurant specializes in snacks and dishes loved by the Qing imperial family. It is a good place to experience the diet of the Qing emperors and empresses.

The Fangshan menu lists more than 800 dishes, the most famous being the Manchurian and Han Grand Banquet. Since an entire presentation of such a banquet takes at least two days to ingest, Fangshan serves a "Choice Selection" of the whole banquet.

The restaurant's decor is dominated by imperial motifs of the dragon and phoenix. Its painted palace lanterns, bright yellow tablecloths and napkins, and Qing-style porcelain and silver tableware, imprinted with a four-word longevity blessing, all remind one of the imperial palace.

Specialties

Shark's Fin in the Shape of Phoenix Tail 凤尾鱼翅

Golden "Frogs" and Jade Abalone 金蟾玉鲍

Top Officer's Bird's Nest 一品官燕

Braised Prawns 油攒大虾

Gui Gong Fu Restaurant 桂公府

Address: 11 Fangjiayuan Hutong,
Nanxiaojie Street, Chaoyangmennei,
Dongcheng District（东城区朝阳门
内南小街芳园胡同 11 号）
Tel: 65127667, 65131776
Price: average RMB 150 per head
Hours: 11:00 am to 10:00 pm

【Xihu Green Tea with Fried Shrimp
西湖龙井虾仁】

The restaurant is located inside a typical traditional complex with three courtyards in the style of the Qing Dynasty. Though renovated, it still keeps its ancient appearance. There are two centenarian trees in it, one wisteria and the other Chinese flowering crabapple. It is a relaxing experience to have dinner or tea under the ancient trees and take in the tranquility of the old siheyuan house.

The restaurant is known for its tea dishes. Tea Growers' Spring Shipping features "bamboo rafts" made of cucumber and "bags" made of egg membranes that contain "tea leaves" made of chopped seafood and mushrooms. "Lu Yu Brewed Tea" uses Oolong tea as the main ingredient. A small bamboo basket contains steaming Oolong tea leaves, and a small pot hangs from four chopsticks that are crossed together. If not warned, one would mistake the tea leaves as meant for drinking, but they are actually meant to be eaten.

Nutritious Pumpkin Stir-fried with Glutinous Rice-cake, produced in Jiangsu and Zhejiang provinces, and then stewed in meat stock, is not only agreeable

【Gui-gong-fu Fish Specialty Hot-pot 桂府大汤鱼锅】

to the palate but also to the eyes. The Water Chestnuts in Ginger and Honey Syrup is also very good. The restaurant's menu is said to be based on a hand-copied imperial cookbook.

【Lu Yu Brewed Tea 陆羽煮茶】

Specialties

Tea Growers' Spring Shipping 茶农春运

Lu Yu Brewed Tea 陆羽煮茶

Shredded Chicken and Biluochun Tea 风丝碧螺春

Yam with Black Tea and Fruit-juice Sauce 红茶果汁山药

His Honored *Beile's* Dried Bean-curd 贝勒爷豆干

Jinyang Restaurant 晋阳饭庄

Restaurant Information

Address: 241 Zhushikou West Street,
Xuanwu District （宣武区珠市口西大
街 241 号）
Tel: 63031669, 63037636 ext. 100
Price: average RMB 80 per head
Hours: 11:00-14:00, 17:00-21:00

【Naked Oats Noodle 莜面卷】

At this restaurant one should not miss the Crispy Fried Duck. The fried duck is golden yellow in color, with a wafting mouth-watering aroma. When you poke the meat slightly with a fork, it will fall off the bones. Tuck the meat, with a dip of *tianmian* sauce (sweet sauce made of fermented flour) and a few scallion shreds, into a thin pancake and take a bite. It's simply delicious.

Stir-fried Buoyu'r (Fish-shaped Pasta) is another must at Jinyang. It is a combination of vegetables

【Fried Mushroom with Garlic 蒜烧苔蘑】

【Steamed Mandarin Fish 清蒸活桂鱼】

and staple. The first step to making boyu'r is using chopsticks to shape the flour paste into three-inch-long strips, which are flipped, one after another, into a pot of boiling water. When the little flour "fish" are done, they are removed from the pot and stir-fried with an assortment of fresh vegetables. The dish is colorful and shiny with vegetable oil, while tasting delectably slippery and chewy.

The restaurant was converted from the former courtyard residence of Ji Xiaolan, a famous Qing-dynasty official and man of letters. It features a small bridge,

a stream, winding corridors, and paintings and calligraphic works by famous artists.

Specialties

Knife-whittled Noodles 刀削面

Cat's-ear Pasta 猫耳朵

Shredded Pork and Sliced Bean Jelly 肉丝温粉皮

Happy Cake 闻喜饼

Crispy Fried Duck 香酥鸭

【Crispy Fried Duck 香酥鸭】

【Moshu Pasta 木须拨鱼】

【Happy Cake 闻喜饼】

Lai Jin Yu Xuan 来今雨轩

Restaurant Information

Address: inside Zhongshan Park, west of Tian'anmen Gate（天安门西侧中山公园内）

Tel: 66056670

Price: RMB 2,500-5,000 for a Red Mansions Banquet (for 10 persons)

Payment: cash or credit card

Hours: 9:00 am to 9:00 pm

【Chicken Skin and Shrimp Ball Soup 鸡皮虾丸汤】

The restaurant has a classic Chinese name, as well as a classic Chinese architecture and environment, being located inside a compound in Zhongshan Park. In the yard grow flowers, grass and Chinese crabapple trees that blossom with white flowers. The waitresses, clad in traditional red *qipao* or cheongsams, add a finishing touch to the picturesque environment. A covered stairway leads one to a high point that opens to a green vista of the park.

In the early 1980s, the restaurant's chefs studied carefully *A Dream of Red Mansions*, particularly the large number of recipes the classic novel describes, and compiled its "Red Mansions Cuisine." Now every dish on the restaurant menu tells a "Red Mansions" story. Red Mansions Cuisine uses nature-blessed and green ingredients, and every one of its dishes is nutritious and good for the body.

【Red Mansion Shredded Egg-plant 茄鲞】

Specialties

Chicken Skin and Shrimp Ball Soup
鸡皮虾丸汤

Black Dragon Playing with a Ball
乌龙戏球

Longevity Blessing from Yihong
Mansion 怡红祝寿

Steamed Buns with Preserved
Chinese Cabbage 茄鲞

Mei Mansion 梅府家宴

Restaurant Information

Address: 24 Daxiangfeng Hutong,
Houhainanyan （后海南沿大翔凤胡
同 24 号）
Tel: 66126845
Price: RMB 200-1,500 per head
Payment: cash or credit card
Hours: 10:30 am to 11:00 pm

Tucked in the depths of Daxiangfeng Hutong in the Houhai (Back Lake) neighborhood, it is a fancy home tavern that serves meals in the family banquet style of famed Peking Opera artist Mei Lanfang. The restaurant has no menu, and diners do not need to bother about what to order. They just decide how much they want to spend, and leave everything else to their "host."

The Mei Mansion is an old building, as evidenced by the 240-year-old jujube tree in the courtyard and the stone hitching post that dates to the Ming Dynasty in the backyard. The dining compartments around the courtyard are decorated with old photographs, gramophones, and old Shanghai furniture of the 1920s and 1930s. Introductions to dishes are written on folding fans.

As demanded by Mei Lanfang's profession, Mei family cuisine stayed away from food that could increase weight while favoring ingredients good for the throat and skin. Mei-family-style Chicken Porridge is stewed over a low fire for 48 hours — until the chicken meat becomes pasty — before vegetable juice is poured over the porridge to form a white and green *Taiji* pattern. This porridge was said to be a must for Mei Lanfang before every performance. Both the home cuisine and elegant siheyuan courtyard house contribute to an unforgettable dining experience.

Specialties

Mei-family-style Chicken Porridge
鸳鸯鸡粥

Deep-fried and Braised Mandarin Fish 浇汁鳜鱼

【Mei Mansion Speciality 梅府菜】

【Bamboo Cucumber 脆竹】

Red Capital 新红资

Address: 66 Dongsijiutiao, Dongcheng
District（东城区东四九条 66 号）
Tel: 64027151/2 (daytime Mon.
through Fri.); 84018886 (nights &
weekends)
Price: RMB 200-300 per herd
Payment: cash
Hours: 6:00-11:00 pm (closed on
Sunday)

【Dragon in Repose 黄瓜龙】

The Red Capital Club is located inside a 200-year-old
siheyuan, whose black-tiled
roofs and vermilion gate do not
distinguish it from other courtyard residences, except for the
1970s vintage Red Flag limo that
is parked in front of the gate.
Motivated by his love for Chinese culture, the proprietor of
the restaurant has turned an old
siheyuan house into a classic
Chinese restaurant that serves
"Zhongnanhai" and imperial
style cuisines.

The Red Capital menu reflects
Chinese history of the latter half
of the 20th century: it is com-

posed of dishes that were loved by former state leaders, and there is a story behind every dish. The restaurant's master chefs, led by a former chef of a past Chinese state leader, magically transform familiar homemade dishes into culinary delicacies.

Apart from its specialties, Red Capital serves red and white wines custom-made in Bordeaux, and an after-dinner Red Capital cigar for some customers further enriches the Red Capital experience.

The restaurant is a living duplicate of 1950s Zhongnanhai. It is furnished entirely with old furniture that was once used by previous state leaders at Zhongnanhai. All its sofas — worn out at edges — are the very Russian-style vintages that once lined the meeting rooms of Zhongnanhai. Three large Chinese characters,

【Spring Rolls 春卷】

meaning "New Red Capitalist," hang over the door of the main building on the northern side of the courtyard.

The underground air-raid shelter in the courtyard has been turned into a unique compact bar, with decor also reflecting the mood of the early years of the People's Republic. On the wall hang stage props from the ballet *The Red Detachment of Women*. One of its corners is occupied by an old film projector and a pile of Chinese name cards.

【Eggplant of Red Mansions 红楼梦茄盒】

Specialties

Dragon in Repose 黄瓜龙

Eggplant of Red Mansions 红楼梦茄盒

Gongbao Shrimp 官爆虾

Spring Rolls 春卷

Manchurian Hunt 满族芝麻鹿肉

Tian Di Yi Jia Restaurant

天地一家

Restaurant Information

Address: 140 Nanchizi Street,
Dongcheng District（东城区南池子
大街 140 号）
Parking: available
Price: average RMB 300 per head
Payment: cash, credit card or check
Hours: 11:00 to 2:00 pm; 5:00-9:00 pm

【 Assorted Meats & Seafood Hotpot Party 火锅】

Five meters north of the Nanchizi Street archway on the east side of the Palace Museum, one will find a big gray-brick courtyard house by the side of the former imperial archives. The plaque over its gate bears four Chinese characters, "*Tian Di Yi Jia*," or "Heaven and Earth Are of One Family." Its dim lighting makes it nothing like habitually showy and noisy Chinese restaurants. In the center of the hall is a big round table, circled by water. Four sacred pillars of the Blue Dragon (east), White Tiger (west), Linnet (south) and Black Tortoise (north) stand on the side of the direction they signify. The dark-gray walls are hung with duplicates of ancient paintings done by renowned artists. Chinese-style tables and chairs of a simple and lineal beauty, tailor-made curtains, primitive stone carvings, terracotta figures and antique cabinets adorn the simple space of the restaurant, endowing it with an air of aristocratic luxury.

The restaurant merges the best of various Chinese and Western cuisines. Diners can taste within one meal, authentic Beijing, Shandong, Jiangsu, Zhejiang, Chaozhou and Guangdong dishes, as well as imperial and aristocratic delicacies, such as abalone, shark's fin, bird's nest, kidney-bean rolls, and pea jelly.

【Braised Abalone & Shark's Fin with Brown Sauce 古法干烧大鲍翅】

【Truffles with Layered Deep-fried Bean-curd 松露千层豆腐】

【Bird's Nest with Egg-white-sauce 芙蓉炒血燕】

Specialties

Sake-marinated Foie Gras 清酒鹅肝

Kobe Beef Roll 神户牛肉卷

Golden-white-ear Fungus Braised with Seasonal Vegetables 黄耳烩时蔬

Ritan Inn House 日坛会馆

【Royal Fo-tiao-qiang, Steamed Assorted Meats in Chinese Casserole 御用坛坛香】

Restaurant Information

Address: Ritan Park (southwestern corner), Chaoyang District（朝阳区日坛公园西南角）

Tel: 65919519

Price: average RMB 300 per person

Parking: RMB 40 (reservation required)

Payment: cash or credit card

Hours: 10:00 am to 11:00 pm

Ritan Inn House is a compound courtyard that sits quietly in the midst of the ancient buildings of the former imperial temple dedicated to the moon. Following a landscaped path through to its rear courtyard, diners will find themselves inside the beautiful Ritan Park. The restaurant decor blends tradition into modernity. On its walls are traditional Chinese paintings done in fine brushwork, and its furnishing reminds one of an imperial home.

Apart from imperial-style dishes, the restaurant also serves Guangdong cuisine and French Tepanyaki. The wonderful taste of its dishes reveals the great amount of time and care that the restaurant puts into cooking as an art. The restaurant has extra-large private rooms. Diners can have an imperial-style dinner in one of them, or spend a wonderful night at the Beer Garden in its courtyard.

Specialties

Top-class Braised Shark's Fin

顶级黄焖翅

Pigeon and Bird's Nest Stew

秘制鸽吞燕

Roast Duck 烤鸭

Venison 鹿肉

【Top-class Braised Shark's Fin 顶级黄焖翅】

Princess Mansion 格格府

Restaurant Information

Address: 9 Big Qudeng Hutong,
behind the National Art Museum of
China, Dongcheng District（东城区
美术馆后街大取灯胡同 9 号内）
Tel: 64078006
Price: RMB 80 per head
Payment: cash or credit card
Hours: 11:00 am to 2: 00 pm; 5:00-
10:00 pm

The eatery's site, a courtyard in the Big Qudeng Hutong in Dongcheng District, was formerly the residence of a Qing-dynasty princess, and is therefore known as "Princess Mansion." The food is a combination of imperial soups with homey hotpots. The former are dedicated to regimen, while the latter are designed for merry group dining and hearty communion.

The rooms are adorned in a stately elegance. Attendants are clad in gorgeous Qing-dynasty costumes, as are the performers in the live show. Cupping a bowl of hot soup in my hands and watching the dancing snow-flakes outside the windows, I was enamored with the sensual and visual beauty of the Chinese courtyard lifestyle. It was the second time that I spent the lunar New Year in Beijing, and this was one of the most wonderful experiences in my life.

Specialties:

Cordyceps and Duck Pot
虫草全鸭炖锅
Chinese Angelica and Black-bone
Chicken Soup 当归乌骨鸡汤
Three in One Pot 三合一炖锅

Simple Health Maintenance Exercises

● Combing the hair: Comb your hair many or even 100 times a day, using a comb or simply your fingers. Combing massages the scalp, which helps alleviate a woozy head. It is also good for one's vision and hearing.

● Drumming the ears: Press tightly on both ears with your palms for a few seconds, before suddenly letting go your hands, so your eardrums will vibrate. This method helps slow down the degeneration of the ears. Regularly massaging or plucking or flicking ears can help alleviate headache, carsickness and other physical unfitness. For people of weak health, massaging the ears often can help prevent colds.

● Massaging the eyes: Massaging your eyes and sockets using the soft part of your palms can enhance local area blood circulation, which is good for the eyes and brain, as well as the skin around your eyes.

● Nipping the nose: Massaging with your two index fingers the *yingxiang* acupuncture points on each side of the nasal bone, or regularly nipping your nose, can enhance your olfaction and reduce chances of nasal allergy and respiratory infection.

● Knocking teeth: Knocking your upper and lower teeth lightly against one another, or making chewing movements can help slow

down gum degeneration and prevent tooth disease. The movement also helps exercise the cheek muscles and prevent the cheek from sagging.

● Swallowing: Close your month, make gargling movement a few times, and then swallow saliva, which has a sweet taste rather than odorous when it is not exposed to air and goes through oxidation. Saliva is rich in digestive enzymes and nutritious elements. It is good for digestion.

● Turning the head and thrusting the shoulders: The neck and shoulders are where the spine is located and rich with blood vessels that go to the head. Regularly turning the head and thrusting the shoulders can help exercise muscles and joints and stimulate blood circulation, which will significantly reduce chances of cerebrovascular diseases when one gets older.

● Dry-rubbing: Rubbing with your palms or a dry towel your face, arms and other exposed parts of your body can help improve epidermal circulation and nourish the skin.

● Patting the shoulders: Swing the left hand upward to pat the right shoulder, and then the right hand to pat the left shoulder. Repeat the movement. You can also pat your thighs with your palms in turns.

● Bending the waist: Bend your waist and try to reach your left toe with your right hand, and straighten up. Then bend again to reach your right toe with your left hand. Repeat the movements several times.

● Clenching the fingers: Close your palms and then stretch out. Repeat several times. The exercise can be done while sitting or standing.

● Stepping on the toes: Use your left heel to step on your right toes, and right heel to step on your left toes. Repeat several times.

Vegetarian Vibrancy

A meat-free diet inspires rather than impairs the physical sinew, and refines one's thoughts. Eco-friendly diners enjoy greater peace and joy at heart, and have deeper insight into the cycles of life. They can therefore remain more upbeat whatever situations they find themselves in.

Baihe Vegetarian Restaurant
百合素食

Restaurant Information

Address: 50 m from the new Jiangong
Gate of the Summer Palace, on the
east side of the road, Haidian District
(海淀区颐和园新建宫门南 50 米路东)
Tel: 62878726
Price: average RMB 50-80 per head
Payment: cash
Hours: 10:30 to 2:00 pm;
5:00-9:30 pm

Baihe is a vintage name in the vegetarian restaurant business in Beijing. The home-based restaurant is always crowded with diners; and the new outlet, standing by a lotus pond outside the Summer Palace, attracts even more diners with its tranquil and beautiful environment. The new restaurant runs a free weekend class for children on Chinese classics.

The restaurant is famed for its

vegetarian cuisine, particularly "chicken drumsticks," "fish" and "pork" made of soybean protein and Amorphophallus Konjac.

The restaurant also provides a unique and beautiful environment where diners can enjoy their food while admiring the lush flowers and plants, works of art and antiques around them. The restaurant often hosts free lectures on Chinese culture.

【Sweet and Sour "Ribs" 糖醋素排】

Specialties

Pineapple and Jackfruit 菠萝菠萝蜜

Garden Noodles with Green Sauce
来自花园的青酱面

"Pork" Stir-fried with Fungus
木耳小炒肉

Rose Banksia 木香水转弯
(Fragrant Wood and Winding Stream)

Black Fungus Soup 上汤黑木耳

Handmade Biscuits 手工饼干

Sichuan-style Crispy "Chicken"
蜀香脆椒鸡

Sweet and Sour "Ribs" 糖醋素排

"Shark's Fin" in a Bamboo Tube
竹筒鱼刺

【Black Fungus Soup 上汤黑木耳】

【Vegetarian Hotpot 素食火锅】

【Rose Banksia 木香水转弯】

Cihai Suxin 慈海素心

Restaurant Information

Address: 103 Di'a nmen West Street, Xicheng District (西城区地安门西大街 103 号齐鲁饭店院内)

Tel: 66571898

Price: average RMB 80 per head

Payment: cash or credit card

Hours: 9:30 am - 11:00 pm

【Bag-shaped Braised Japanese Tofu Stuffed with Prawns 布袋豆腐】

Cihai Suxin provides busy urban residents with a quiet, spacious setting, with subtle Buddhist music playing in the background, for the enjoyment of delightful vegetarian dishes made from choice ingredients.

The place is divided into a vegetarian restaurant and a teahouse. The former adopts its name from "Bodhi Garden" (implying "awareness and consummation"), with simple yet elegant decor. With its curtains made from linden beads, the restaurant has a large hall but maintains each table's dining privacy. Its divine interior decoration of

Buddhist murals and scriptures gives diners a dualistic experience, physical and spiritual. The teahouse is aptly named as "Sounds of the Sea" (implying "extraordinary spaciousness"). In the teahouse are large bookshelves, an open-style bar, glass curtains, a variety of teas, and exquisite tea sets. All these create a comfortable and quiet place for patrons to appreciate tea, converse with friends, while enjoying the sounds of nature.

【Streaky Pork and Corn 多聚财宝】

Specialties

Greentech Red Sausages on Bamboo Leaf 一指禅

Bag-shaped Braised Japanese Tofu Stuffed with Prawns 布袋豆腐

Streaky Pork and Corn 多聚财宝

"Duck" with Tofu-wrapped Salted Cabbage and Mushrooms 慈海素烤鸭

【"Duck" with Tofu-wrapped Salted Cabbage and Mushrooms 慈海素烤鸭】

【Fungus Dance with Bamboo Shoots 松茸与竹笋】

Lotus Pond in Moonlight
荷塘月色

Restaurant Information

Address: No. 12 Building, Liufang Nanli, Chaoyang District（朝阳区柳芳南里12号楼）

Tel: 64653299, 64663114

Price: average RMB 50 per head

Payment: cash or credit card

Hours: 10:00 am to 2:00 pm; 5:00-9:00 pm

Lotus blossoms are the first thing that catches one's eyes on entering this poetically named place. The floor is quaintly uneven due to the multiplicity of patterns on it. Every table is elegantly covered, adorned with a pink flower curving from a vase.

The French windows in the sunlight-drenched corridor offer natural views. When a pot of "Back to Shangri-La," an amber-colored beverage of light

【Spicy Vegetarian "Beef" with Vegetarian "Fish and Ham" 水煮三国】

【Vegetarian "Steak" with Broccoli and Black Pepper Sauce 黑椒墨玉】

fragrance, is brought to the table, the mind flashes back to lovely scenes from poems read many years ago. A meal here nourishes not only the body but the soul as well.

【Vegetarian Sushi 北海道晚餐】

【Herbal Combination with Linden Leaves and Flowers 菩提树下饮甘露】

Specialties

Vegetarian Sushi 北海道晚餐

Herbal Combination with Linden Leaves and Flowers 菩提树下饮甘露

Tofu-wrapped Vegetarian "Meat" 云中锦书

Vegetarian "Steak" with Broccoli and Black Pepper Sauce 黑椒墨玉

Spicy Vegetarian "Beef" with Vegetarian "Fish and Ham" 水煮三国

【Traditional Chinese Corn-flour Cakes 田园野趣】

【Tofu-wrapped Vegetarian "Meat" 云中锦书】

Pure Lotus Vegetarian Restaurant 净心莲

Address: 3rd Floor, Holiday Inn Lido
Beijing, 6 Jiangtai Road（将台路 6 号
丽都假日饭店 3 层）

Tel: 64376688

Price: average RMB 120 per head

Payment: cash or credit card

Hours: 09:30-24:00

【Brown Rice 糙米饭】

Pure Lotus provides a cozy and elegant dining ambience. The restaurant is furnished with cane tables and chairs adorned by green silk cushions with butterfly designs. The white gauze curtains, offset by pinkish ones, also have butterfly motifs. Pots of Alocasia rhizome decorate the dining area, and inkwash paintings of lotus hang from the walls. Buddhist artifacts and other ornaments are displayed harmoniously to enhance the grace and serenity of the environment.

An agreeable environment and carefully prepared food contribute to a pleasant dining experience. Though the portions are not large, every dish represents the sincerity of the proprietor. The Cool Mountain Mushroom uses autumn mushrooms from the Wutai Mountains. It is very delicious and helps enhance blood circulation. Jackfruit with Crisp Lotus Root is also most tempting.

Specialties

Roast Vegetarian Sausage 烤肠

Vegetarian Sausage Casserole
干锅肥肠

Boiled "Fish" 水煮鱼

Black Pepper "Ribs" 黑椒圆排

Moonlit Lotus Pond with Lily Aroma
荷塘月色百合香

【Green Rolls 素手卷】

【Mix Vegetable With Cheese 面包焗时蔬】

Xuxiangzhai Vegetarian Restaurant 叙香斋

Restaurant Information

Address: A26-1 Guozijian Street,
Dongcheng District（东城区国子监
大街甲 26-1 号）
Tel: 64046568
Price: average RMB 60 per head
Payment: cash or credit card
Hours: 11:00 am to 10:00 pm

【Assorted Lotus Vegetarian Mix with Buddhism
Creativity 佛法无边】

Xuxiangzhai mainly offers a vegetarian buffet. Located in the vicinity of the famous Yonghegong Lama Temple, the restaurant is nestled in a beautiful environment of ancient trees, vermilion walls and green-tiled roofs. In harmony with its environment, the restaurant is decorated in classic Chinese style with Buddhist touches. Confucianism is also part of its corporate culture, with most of its staff members well informed in classics of Confucius and Mencius.

Xuxiangzhai cuisine promotes

【Brazil Morel 巴西炒羊肚菌】

【Dynasty Supreme Abalone 官府一品鲍】

nature-blessed and healthy food. Its culinary arts emphasize color, aroma, appearance and taste, while maintaining the nutritious elements of ingredients.

Since the restaurant opened its RMB58 buffet, it has won over a large customer base. The buffet features not only traditional vegetarian dishes, but also Japanese cuisine, southern and northern Chinese snacks and desserts, as well as Western-style salads and icecreams.

Specialties

Clover Rolls 苜蓿芽手卷

Boiled "Pork Slices" Sauteed in Hot Sauce 虎掌回锅肉

Shish Kebabs 罗汉羊肉串

【Shish Kebabs 罗汉羊肉串】

【Sweet Black Rice Jelly 参汁黑米露】

【Alfalfa Sprouts Rolls 苜蓿芽手卷】

Everyday Secrets to Robustness

Breakfast: Have breakfast to replenish cellulose, and eat lots of fruit.

Red wine: Wine helps adjust cholesterol levels, prevent blood coagulation and reduce the chances of heart disease. Red wine is rich in antioxidants, so taking some red wine while eating is good for the body.

More vegetables and fruits than meat: Control of calorie intake can help slow down the aging process.

Gastronomy: Good eating brings pleasant sensations to both the body and the mind, and good mood will enhance the function of your immune system.

Physical exercise: One should spend at least an hour a week on demanding exercises, such as jogging and climbing either a hill or a stairway. Such exercises can help strengthen one's health and enhance myocardial and cardiovascular functions.

Dancing: Learn dances, such as belly, Latin, International Standard dancing and more, to experience their magic as well as that of music and other cultures. Dancing will maintain one's passion and love for life.

Pet-raising: Raising a pet is a type of enforced exercise, since the owner has to take it out for regular exercise.

Adequate sleeping: High-quality sleeping can help the body generate more growth hormones, which is the most important chemical element against aging. Taking a nap every day will not only enhance your daily performance but also help prolong your lifespan.

● Making friends: A broad range of interests and activities will help you make more friends, and more friends mean more channels for relieving mental stress.

● Happy family life: Generally speaking, people who have a spouse live longer than single people. Quality sex life is good for both physical and mental health.

● Traveling: A broad view of the world will enhance your physical and mental health.

● Smiling: Smiling helps exercise your whole body by relaxing muscles, improving blood circulation, reducing high blood pressure and strengthening the immune system.

● Maintaining curiosity and continuing to learn: One will stay brain-active and young by studying new things.

● Training an artistic mind: Beautiful music will free one from worldly worries and stress. Developing an inclination for art and music will take you into a world of genuine feeling, benevolence and beauty, as well as inspire your passion for life.

● Learning about your physical well-being: Prevention is better than cure. People should know about their own bodies and take preventive treatments, or the earliest possible treatment therapies, to avoid deterioration of their physical condition.

Postscript

My continuing adventure with the culinary arts has changed my life. Wandering around Beijing in search of delicacies from across the world has been a process of fun and enlightenment that has led me to the true beauty and meaning of life.

Like many people I used to be lost in the pursuit of a better material life, commuting between commercial centers from 9 am to 8 pm every day, experiencing jitters with the fluctuations in the international stock market, and caring about nothing more than the figures in the company's financial reports. Clients' investment plans always took priority to my own fitness plan, and shares going higher was more desirable than enjoying the world's best cuisines. My endeavors did pay off, as I took the post of vice-president of ABN AMRO Bank at the age of 31, but this was achieved at the cost of my health.

I was laid low by severe sciatica in 2002. In the following two years I could barely stand when the pain hit, not to mention taking a step anywhere. The illness ravaged my health, but also turned around my understanding of living. Life is ruled by karma. One gains, one pays. Excessive work in the early years cuts into one's muscle preservation, and devours the share that could maintain one in good shape in later years. Those who presume they can defy the limits of the human body will witness the bitter results sooner or later. As a saying goes: people have the right to use but not to own their lives. Be good to yourself, and remain physically and psychologically sound, or you will not be able to find real happiness in life.

From that time on, I vowed to give myself another chance to fully enjoy my life. I cannot change the environment, but I can change my own habits to build up good health. I cannot determine the length of my life, but I can expand its dimensions through study. I cannot alter others' judgments, but I can adopt a new attitude toward life.

In the darkest days of my illness I searched through my mind for unfulfilled dreams. The first was to travel around the world. Given the numbers, 224 countries and regions on Earth, I saw little hope of visiting them all by the age of 60 if I managed to travel to two each year. Then the goal of trying all the cuisines in the world seemed more realistic.

With this idea, I have since never hurried through each meal as I used to, but experienced it with my heart. In fact I don't take anything for granted anymore, and instead spend every day with enjoyment and gratitude.

A closer look at life has invigorated my desire for more knowledge. And the study of different arts, such as music and dance, has nourished both my soul and my body. These efforts are the best investments I have made in my life.

Acknowledgement

I hope I may be able to help some people by sharing my experiences with them. And I feel most grateful to those who helped me in completing this book.

My thanks go to, first of all, the Foreign Languages Press, my tutors and friends whose frequent visits to Beijing prompted me to follow the latest in the city's food-service sector, and diplomats of foreign embassies and staff of foreign chambers of commerce in Beijing, whose instruction has broadened my insight into diverse international cuisines. I must also express gratitude to Mr. Wei Zhiyuan and his wife Chen Xi, along with Chen Jun, and professors and students of the Guanghua School of Management of Peking University. The following is the list of people to whose assistance I owe this book:

Christopher Zhuang, Tina, Teresa, Gonger, Chunyan, Ling, Celine, Heidi, Victor, Elmer, Annie, Kevin, Pauline, Maggie, Qiyuan, Edith, Steven, Da-wei, Juliet, Wealey, Joe, Roger, Sunny, Mr. Hwang Gyu Gwang, Alice, Larry, Hallenye, Louisa, Sophie, Dr. Xie De-yong, Dr. Hsieh Qin-liang, Dr. Xu Mei-lu, Suime, Mary, Allen, Karl, Eddy, Rico, Rita, Vivien, Flora, Ruby, Portia, Ricky, Ovid, Vincy, Zhou Xi, Xiao Long, and Yoyo.

I would also like to thank my family — my parents, my husband Nick Wang and my son Kevin Wang — for their full-hearted love and support. They have accompanied me along the roads and lanes across Beijing in search of distinctive restaurants, both empowering me and witnessing my growth.

At last I have to express my appreciation to my readers. The eagerness to share with you the joy and beauty in life motivated me to complete this book. I hope it will be able to inspire you to explore the wonders of good food and life as well. Remember, be healthy and happy. You can begin to work toward this end from any moment, and see the changes in your life.

In the process of working on this book I came to the understanding that we discover what is most precious in the world not with our eyes but rather with our hearts.

Enjoy good food, and have a great day!

图书在版编目（CIP）数据

世界美食在北京：英文 ／ 李幸娟著；孙雷等译

—北京：外文出版社，2008

ISBN 978-7-119-05466-7

Ⅰ．世… Ⅱ．①李… ②孙… Ⅲ．餐厅－简介－北京市－英文

Ⅳ．F719.3

中国版本图书馆 CIP 数据核字（2008）第 118611 号

世界美食在北京

作　　者：李幸娟

英文翻译：孙　雷　汪光强　周晓刚　冯　鑫

英文审定：May　Yee　王明杰

责任编辑：杨　璐

装帧设计：北京华子图文设计公司

印刷监制：张国祥

© 2008 外文出版社

出　　版：外文出版社

　　　　　中国北京西城区百万庄大街 24 号

　　　　　邮政编码：100037

　　　　　网　　址：http://www.flp.com.cn

　　　　　电　　话：008610－68320579（总编室）

　　　　　　　　　　008610－68995852（发行部）

　　　　　　　　　　008610－68327750（版权部）

印　　制：北京外文印刷厂

开　　本：787mm × 1092mm　1/32

印　　张：8.5

2008 年第 1 版第 1 次印刷

（英）

ISBN 978-7-119-05466-7

09800（装别）

85-E-662P